50 Amazing Swiss Women

True Stories You Should Know About

Dedications

To my mother Heidi, my sister Sibylle, and my daughter Hannah – three sensational Swiss women! (AL)

To Asier, for always pushing me towards my dreams. To all the amazing women in my life – we stand together, proud of who we are and what we've done, ready to lift the next generation of women even higher. (AN)

To Andy, Julia, mom and dad for always believing in me. In memory of Nelly, Silvia, *Grossmami* and *Grossmüetti*, amazing Swiss women whose strength inspired me. (BN)

To my daughters, Emma and Elodie, who are growing up to be the most amazing Swiss women. (KH)

To Sue Delarue – my Californian mother, and grandmother to my two amazing young Swiss women. (LT)

To all those stubborn women who still inspire me every day. To my mother Eliane and my grandmother, Jeanne. In memory of my godmother, Jocelyne. (ML)

FSC www.fsc.org
MIX
Paper from responsible sources
FSC® C014138

50 Amazing Swiss Women: True Stories You Should Know About ISBN 978-3-03869-104-4

The Schwabe Publishing Group (Bergli Books, NZZ Libro, and Zytglogge Verlag) is being supported by the Swiss Federal Office of Culture for the years 2021–2024.

Also published in German as *50 sensationelle Schweizerinnen: Geschichten, die du kennen solltest*
978-3-03869-105-1
Also published in French as *50 Suissesses sensationnelles: des histoires vraies à découvrir*
978-3-03869-106-8

Printed in the Czech Republic

www.bergli.ch

50 Amazing Swiss Women

True Stories You Should Know About

By
Laurie Theurer
Katie Hayoz
Anita Lehmann
Alnaaze Nathoo
and
Barbara Nigg

Illustrated by
Mireille Lachausse

50 Amazing Swiss Women

Welcome

When I first set out to write a book about amazing Swiss women, I thought that I would need to search far and wide for inspirational stories. How wrong I was! They are everywhere. The more I looked, the more I found. Before I knew it, I had a list of names that was far longer than I could ever hope to research, interview, and write about by myself. It was time to assemble an author team.

The five of us got to work, researching women of the past and interviewing women of the present. As we progressed, we noticed something remarkable. Most of these women, who we found admirable and inspirational in so many ways, did not seem to think of themselves as such. They were simply people who were following their hearts and their passions, completely unaware of how fascinating their lives were! In my mind, that was the best reason yet for including them all in this book.

The women who appear in this book are not the 'fifty best women' we found. They are a beginning – a collection of fifty marvelous and diverse women who we agreed belonged in this first volume. There are so many more individuals whose stories also deserve to be told. We encourage you to reach out to us on social media to let us know about even more fabulous Swiss women.

I hope the stories we've selected for *50 Amazing Swiss Women: True Stories You Should Know About* delight and inspire you. I hope they show the power, diversity, and ingenuity of these remarkable people. I hope they show you how many different ways there are for all of us – including you! – to be amazing.

Laurie Theurer
January 2021
Instagram: 50_amazing__swiss_women
Facebook: @50amazingswisswomen

Nina Burri

The Woman Who Twists Her Way Into Our Hearts

Born 1977

Nina Burri remembers the moment when she first sat on her own head. She laid on her stomach, reached behind her back and pulled her feet up until her bottom rested on the back of her head. The 'headsit' was one of the most difficult contortion poses to perform. But she could finally do it!

Never a stranger to hard work and discipline, Nina started ballet lessons when she was six. Although neither of her parents were performers, they sent her to ballet schools in her hometown of Bern, in Basel and eventually in Graz, Austria. The ballet world was demanding, the competition was fierce and instructors expected perfection. Nina made lots of mistakes and her instructors were very hard on her. Nina had to re-learn many of the moves, and then do them over and over again. By 2000, when Nina was dancing professionally for the *Staatstheater Saarbruecken* in Germany, she'd realised that the dancing world was far too demanding – and had stolen much of her self-confidence.

It was time to re-define herself. Nina had always loved the circus. She dreamt of creating a solo act where she could combine ballet with elements of acrobatics. A whole new kind of show!

Some of the best acrobatic schools are in China, so off she went to train at the China Acrobatic Troupe in Beijing. For six months, she took courses in acrobatics, contortion and even learned Chinese. As a thirty-year-old Swiss woman from Bern, she was by far the oldest student. Her classmates were mostly children and circus performers who had practiced acrobatics and contortion all their lives. Nina had started practicing only two months before, twisting and stretching her body for up to eight hours per day just to keep up.

Nina worried that her 'older' body's aches and pains would make her quit. But as her contortion training continued, she found the movements actually felt great!

Nina returned to Switzerland at the end of 2007, ready to create a dance and contortion act that no other Swiss person could possibly match. Her confidence in herself and her abilities returned. She competed in talent shows in Switzerland, France and the USA and became known far and wide as the 'Snake Lady'. She's performed in the circus, acted in films, and modelled for *Vogue*.

In 2018, Nina released a photobook titled *Body in Motion* that showcases both the natural beauty of the human body and the amazing things it can do – as well as Nina's newfound confidence in her own remarkable form of art.

'Do what you always wanted, and don't ask others for approval!'

Marie Heim Vögtlin

The Woman Who Became a Doctor Against All Odds

1845–1916

Anywhere she went in the University of Leipzig – the lecture hall, the operating room, the clinic – Marie Vögtlin couldn't escape the whistles, boos and insults. In 1873, as the only female student among 3,700 men, she was bullied and harassed, even during classes. Often, it got so bad that professors had her listen to lectures from a connecting room with the door open.

Six years earlier, Marie had been doing all her work behind closed doors. In Bözen, Aargau, in the late hours of the night while her father slept, twenty-one-year-old Marie secretly studied Latin, mathematics and sciences. She knew her father wouldn't approve, but Marie intended to get into medical school.

In 1867, the University of Zurich first allowed women to attend classes, but those who did so were all foreigners. The following year when Marie announced her intentions, there was there an uproar. A Swiss woman wanted to go to university! To be a doctor! Articles appeared in newspapers calling her criminal and mentally unstable. They said women were too weak-minded to learn medicine. Marie was about to prove them all wrong.

Though at first he was hesitant, her father ended up fully supporting Marie. Even though she was an adult, she was also a woman, and needed his permission to study. Thanks to his support, she was admitted to the University of Zurich in 1868. She completed her medical studies, then went on to specialise in gynaecology (women's health) by training in Leipzig, Germany. Despite being harassed and taunted there, she never gave up. Marie officially became Switzerland's first female doctor in 1874.

She could not receive a permit to practice medicine, however, until, once again, her father gave his consent. Marie then opened a gynaecological office in Zurich. Her dedication and her keen desire to help all women, from the poorest to the richest, made her immensely popular. Women would line up outside her practice early in the morning. They would take their lunch, as often the line was long enough that they might be waiting for hours. Wealthy women even paid poorer women to keep their spots in line for them!

Despite her success, because she was a woman, Zurich authorities still treated her as a child. When she got married in 1875, her husband had to give written approval for her to keep working as a doctor! Marie had two children and continued working, despite societal pressure to do otherwise.

In 1901, Marie helped found the first women's clinic and nursing school in Switzerland. The clinic was for women, and was run and staffed by women. For decades Marie fought so that women could learn medicine in the lecture hall alongside the other students – where they belonged.

'I handle my scalpel as easily as my sewing needle.'

Abassia Rahmani

The Woman Who Is the First Female Blade Runner in Switzerland

Born 1992

The crowd cheered as Abassia flew down the track at the 2016 Paralympic Games in Rio de Janeiro. Still new to running on blades, she surged past one sprinter, then another, and another. Nobody had expected she'd get into the finals. But here she was.

Growing up in Wila, Zurich, Abassia enjoyed sports, but her dream was to become a flight attendant. Then, when she was sixteen, she caught meningitis, a deadly bacterial infection. She was in so much pain, the doctors put her into a coma for six weeks. When she awoke, she found they had amputated her legs below the knees to save her life.

Abassia was devastated to lose her legs. Learning to walk on prosthetic legs was slow and hellish. Her muscles burned and the skin around her stumps was raw after just five minutes. Then, she saw a young man who'd lost both legs above the knee climb the stairs. The metal knees in his prosthetics made going up stairs even harder than it was for her. That's when she thought, 'If he can do it, I can do it!'

Five years later, Abassia heard about a blade running workshop. Heinrich Popow, a Paralympic gold-medal winner, showed her how to run with blades – lightweight, flexible prosthetics built for speed. Trying to run in normal prosthetics was like running in ski boots. With blades, Abassia felt free!

It took Abassia a year to save 14,000Fr. to buy some blades. But she couldn't find anyone in Switzerland who knew how to sprint with them. So, she joined a local track and field club in Winterthur where the coach was keen to help her figure it out. Abassia threw herself into her first competitive race and never looked back.

After two years of competing, she decided to race in Rio, even though she was told by the people around her that she was too ambitious. But that made her want to do it even more! After just three months training for the 200-metre race, Abassia flew across the finish line in just 27.86 seconds to place fourth. She'd made it into the top five and just missed winning a bronze medal on her first try.

After Rio, Abassia quit her part-time job, found sponsors and became a professional athlete, training for up to four hours a day, six times a week. It paid off, as she won the 200-metre race at the Para-Athletics European Championships in 2018.

Now training for the Tokyo Olympics in 2021, Abassia is happier with her body than she ever was before she lost her legs. And today, more Swiss girl amputees are running on blades, flying down the track, full speed ahead.

'Having a disability does not make one inspirational. Hard work, perseverance and determination do.'

Annemarie Schwarzenbach

The Woman Who Dared To Be Herself

1908–1942

It was the 1930s, and the world was changing. Up to that point, Annemarie Schwarzenbach's life had been filled with parties and fun. Now, with fascist and racist ideas growing popular all over the world, she grew upset. It was time to take her passions – writing and photography – and use them in the fight against these evil ideas.

The third of five children, Annemarie was born into one of Zurich's richest families. She was beautiful and fiercely intelligent. Her favorite subjects were history and music, and she always knew she was going to become a writer. When she was twenty-three, she moved to Berlin to devote her life to journalism, and when she was twenty-five, she jumped in her car and went to Turkey, Syria and Persia, and wrote a book about her trip, and included her own photos. She wrote novels, political articles and travelogues about her wild adventures. One even included a car chase with the police in Azerbaijan!

Annemarie also loved taking pictures. She was one of the first photographers who understood that a photo could tell a story – by doing something as simple as writing a short text that would be printed with the picture. For example, she took a photo of a woman on a rock, cutting an apple. But the photo wasn't just that. It told the story of a woman who was about to go to court and face a judge who was against her, and how she was too weak to fight a corrupt justice system.

Annemarie was fearless. All she needed was a car, a typewriter and a camera, and she was ready for anything. In her search to tell people's stories and bring more justice to the world, she took tremendous risks. She documented a march of the Hitler Youth, visited America's racist Deep South and descended into Swedish ore mines.

Despite her wealth and success, Annemarie's life wasn't happy or easy. She was a lesbian – a woman who loved women – and did not hide it. Plus, her political opinions were very different from her parents. She suffered from a constant confrontation between who she was, what she believed in, and what her family expected of her. This led her to battle fear, depression and drug addiction. In an effort to change her, her family forced her into a psychiatric clinic.

When Annemarie died at the age of thirty-four following a bicycle accident, her mother burned all of her personal papers, as she was afraid they would disgrace the family. But Annemarie's stories live on through her writing and her photographs, and what she has left behind is just as important as the life she has lived.

'Terrible uncertainty? Terrible only as long as we can't look it in the eye.'

Carla del Ponte

The Woman Who Scared the Gangsters

Born 1947

In 1989, the Italian mafia planted half a ton of explosives on the very spot where Carla del Ponte was going to meet with a judge in Sicily. Luckily, the explosives were found just in time and could be defused. Carla and the judge did not get blown up, and escaped unscathed. But on Carla's return home, she received an anonymous phone call.

'You saw what's just happened,' said a man's voice. 'Now behave!'

That man clearly didn't know Carla very well.

Carla had grown up in Canton Ticino with three brothers who would go out snake-hunting and put vipers under Carla's bed, hoping to scare her. But knowing that there was a snake under her bed never stopped Carla from sleeping. Later, she wanted to study medicine, like her brothers, but her father thought that such long studies were a waste of time and money – after all, Carla was never going to work as a doctor. She was going to get married and have children!

In the end, Carla chose to study law instead, because she liked the idea of finding justice for victims of crime. She studied in Bern, Geneva and London.

As a Swiss federal prosecutor, Carla led investigations into the Italian Mafia. Later, she became the chief prosecutor for the International Criminal Court in The Hague. Carla investigated war crimes in Yugoslavia, Rwanda and Syria. She listened to the stories of thousands of victims, visited mass graves, read detailed reports about torture and massacres. Carla saw death and suffering all around her, but the more terrible the crime, the more Carla felt spurred on to find justice for the victims. She always went for the big criminals – leaders, generals, presidents – pushing for these people to be tried and put behind bars.

Carla always spoke her mind. She didn't care what anyone thought of her, whether they were colleagues or enemies. She kept digging for evidence, and refused to give up, even when she received death threats. This is why she was nicknamed 'Carla the Pest'.

'Carla the Pest' made mighty enemies. Powerful, rich and well-connected criminals tried to stop her. They shot at Carla in Belgrade, and she escaped an assassination attempt in Sicily. She had bulletproof windows and doors installed in her home and drove an armour-plated car. She couldn't even leave her house without bodyguards. But, just like the vipers under her bed, none of this ever stopped her from sleeping at night – neither the crimes she prosecuted, nor the criminals out to get her.

'I haven't been scared in a long time. ... When it's time to die, it's time to die, and that's it.'

Regula Engel-Egli

The Woman Who Was a Swiss Amazon

1761–1853

The soldier shot one enemy attacker in the face. But more enemies were coming, and before there was time to reload, the soldier was stabbed in the ribs and got a bullet through the neck. At the hospital in Brussels, doctors removed the soldier's uniform to tend to the wounds and found that the soldier … was a woman.

Born in Zurich, Regula Egli learned to fend for herself at a very young age. After her parents separated, her mother returned to her native Graubünden – without Regula. Her father, a mercenary soldier hired to fight battles abroad, had to place Regula in an orphanage for six years. Once her father remarried, Regula often argued with her stepmother, finally running away at thirteen to find her mother. In Graubünden, she met Florian Engel, a Swiss officer in a mercenary army fighting for the French, and married him when she was seventeen.

Regula was now a mercenary officer's wife. So, over the next thirty-seven years, she often marched along with the troops and stayed by Florian's side. By the time of the French Revolution in 1789, she'd already given birth to seven children. When Florian was arrested and jailed in Paris, she took their children along to plead for his life. The French leader Robespierre was so impressed by Regula's brave pleas that he granted Florian's release.

Onwards to Holland, where Regula gave birth to another baby while lying on the ground between two cannons. The following morning, she marched along with the soldiers, baby on her arm and seven more children in tow.

In 1798, Regula and Florian joined Napoleon on his expedition to Egypt, where Regula gave birth to twins. Napoleon, the happy godfather, baptised the babies himself. From Egypt, Regula travelled with the troops to Gaza, Jaffa and Syria. When the troops grew tired, Regula relieved them, dressing in a soldier's uniform and keeping guard. From there, it was only a matter of time until she and her older children joined in the battles. In total, Regula had twenty-one children, all but five of them dying in the battles they fought for France. Napoleon adored her and called her 'my little Swiss woman'.

In 1815, Napoleon's troops lost their final battle at Waterloo, Belgium. Regula lost her husband Florian and two of her sons, and wound up in the Brussels hospital herself. Once she recovered from her injuries, Regula went in search of her five remaining children, travelling all the way to the USA to find one of them. She reached him three days before he died of yellow fever in her arms.

At sixty-two, Regula returned to Zurich to write her memoir, which was snapped up by the public. The royalties weren't enough, though. She died at ninety-two, alone, penniless and mostly forgotten by her country. But her story deserves to live on.

'As gold is tested by fire, so is man tested by suffering.'

Nicole Petignat

The Woman Who Refereed Men's Football

Born 1966

When Nicole Petignat's sister told her, 'I've signed us up for a refereeing course,' Nicole had no clue she was setting out on a path to make history.

As children, Nicole and her twin sister, Dominique, played football with the local boys and watched games with their father. At age sixteen, they tried to create a girls' football team in their hometown of Alle (Canton Jura), but no one was interested. So, they took a refereeing course. If they couldn't play women's games, at least they could officiate men's.

They refereed amateur matches in the Canton Jura for about five years. When Dominique started a family, Nicole moved to Lucerne, working odd jobs to pay the bills while officiating at the weekend. At first, Nicole surprised everyone when she set foot on the field, whistle and watch in hand. But once she worked her way up from officiating amateur leagues to professional leagues, everyone knew who Nicole was. She was a woman in a man's world – and she was the one calling the penalties.

Nicole passed the same written and physical tests male referees took, yet got a lot more scrutiny. When Nicole did something the public liked, they gave her twice the love. But when she did something they didn't like, she got twice the hate.

Her name was listed in magazine articles like 'Top Women Who Annoy Swiss Men'. Spectators shouted, 'Go back to your knitting, Nicole!' Sometimes bodyguards accompanied her to a match. But none of that stopped her. Once she blew that starting whistle, everything else melted away and she was inside the game. There, emotions ran high – from frustration, to anger, to hope, to elation – all of it humming under her skin like a live electrical wire.

Nicole officiated at games all over the world, from the FIFA Women's World Cup, to the women's UEFA Euro, to the women's tournament at the Olympic Games. In 2003, Nicole made history when she was the first woman ever to referee an international men's match at the UEFA Cup.

At the UEFA match, Nicole knew the world was watching. Only thirty minutes into the game, the power in the stadium went out. Play continued in the waning daylight until half-time. Then the electricity came back on … but it was accompanied by a torrential rain. Now Nicole couldn't easily communicate with her assistants because her electronic equipment was wet! Despite all of these obstacles, she officiated like a boss, opening the way for other women to referee at the highest levels.

Nicole had never expected to rise as high as she did. For twenty-four years, she simply took each match as it came, doing her best. Doing it for the love of the game.

'Never give up!'

Emma Jung-Rauschenbach

The Woman Who Was at the Eye of the Storm

1882–1955

When her husband, the brilliant psychiatrist Carl Jung, was rude to their dinner guest yet again, Emma Jung gave her husband a swift kick under the table. Emma was brilliant in her own right … and knew how to keep her famous husband from causing a ruckus.

Emma grew up in one of Switzerland's wealthiest families in an elegant mansion in Basel. Nicknamed Sunny, Emma loved to read about art and nature, spending her days writing and thinking. Emma dreamt of studying at university, but her high place in society made this impossible – it was unthinkable for a lady to sit in a class full of men. But when she met Carl, she realised he appreciated her intelligence and imagination. Although he was sometimes bold and loud, she fell in love with the charming young doctor. Once married, Emma and Carl moved to an apartment above the buzzing wards of Zurich's Bürgholzli Hospital, where he treated mentally ill patients.

Emma loved her exciting new life and worked as Carl's research assistant. She spent time with patients, typed up Carl's reports, and learned 'a thing or two' about a new treatment called 'psychoanalysis'.

Until that time, people with mental illnesses were plunged into freezing ice-cold baths, 'treated' with painful electric-shock therapy and plenty of other tortures. Carl used psychoanalysis, a new 'talk therapy' that focused on talking about a patient's dreams and desires. Emma learned a lot about this therapy while living at the hospital.

In 1905, Emma inherited a fortune when her father died. She and Carl built a large home on Lake Zurich where Carl also saw patients. Emma took care of their five children and managed a very busy household. Determined to keep learning and growing, Emma started seeing patients. Still, on any given day, she might patch up a scraped knee, help kids with homework, entertain people like Albert Einstein and see Carl's patients when he was travelling. Still, she found time to write poetry and teach herself Greek and Latin so she could research material for Carl's famous book *Symbols of Transformation,* which introduced analytical psychology. This new talk therapy helped patients value their inner lives.

In 1916, Emma became the first president of the Psychology Club. She presented her own work in the field of analytical psychology, drawing attention to the problems women face in a society that discouraged their desire to learn and grow. In 1950, she became the president of the Jung Institute, where people still train in analytical psychology today.

Being Carl's wife wasn't always easy for Emma. But she found a way to support him while staying true to herself. Plus, they never stopped learning from each other.

'Women must not languish but lift themselves to dismiss society's denigration.'

Marie-Paule Kieny

The Woman Who Vaccinated Foxes

Born 1955

Waiting in the lab, Marie-Paule Kieny was excited. The first helicopter had just left with cartons filled with fox bait. If their idea worked, the helicopters would come back with foxes. She and her team would be able to give them a new vaccine and save many of them from being killed with poison gas.

Many years before, in 1968, thirteen-year-old Marie-Paule had been inspired by protesters crowding the streets of France. They wanted change. Roads were blocked. Schools were closed. Factories stopped working. Marie-Paule decided that she too was going to find new ways of doing things, better ways – at home and all over the world.

Marie-Paule's family was always very supportive of her dreams. There was only one rule – no laziness! You had to get up and work – and help others. Her mother was a doctor. Her grandmother had been a teacher and the head of a labour union. Her great grandmother, a midwife. At first, Marie-Paule wanted to study agronomy, the science of improving the way people farm, and use what she had learned to help feed people. But when the head of the French Institute for Development came to speak to her class, he said that he didn't want to hire women, because they were not as smart as men. Marie-Paule knew she didn't want to work for men like that.

Instead, Marie-Paule got a PhD in microbiology, the study of living things that are too small to see with just your eyes. She learned how sick wild foxes were killed with poison gas to protect people from the deadly virus rabies. Marie-Paule knew vaccines could save foxes and protect people. The problem was, foxes don't usually line-up to get vaccinated at the doctor's office! That's when Marie-Paule and her team came up with a plan to drop traps from helicopters and vaccinate foxes before releasing them back into the forest.

They treated so many foxes with the new vaccine that there was no longer any need to kill them. It saved animals and people alike!

Marie-Paule soon moved from France to Geneva, working for the World Health Organisation. Her work evolved from vaccinating foxes, to working with governments and scientists to deal with the world's most important health problems, like finding a vaccine for Ebola. No matter what she does, Marie-Paule continues to push forward, with or without a helicopter.

'Be bold and daring, but not arrogant. Be prepared to work hard'

Nadja Schmid

The Woman Who Sows Seeds of Joy

Born 1989

When she was fourteen, Nadja Schmid fell ill with pneumonia. She spent three weeks in hospital. Her coughing got worse and worse. Antibiotics didn't work. Convinced she was dying, the doctors gave up. But Nadja didn't give up. She wanted to live, and eventually recovered. The doctors said it was a miracle, but reckoned that Nadja was unlikely to live beyond twenty. Today, she is thirty, and thriving.

Nadja was born in Cressier, Fribourg with an illness called Spinal Muscular Atrophy, a genetic condition that makes the muscles weaker. Nadja has never been able to walk, and relies on other people to help her for much of her daily life. Despite this, Nadja has always lived by the same rules as everybody else. When school started at 8 am, Nadja was there, along with her able-bodied classmates. She resented being singled out because of her disability and wanted to be treated like everyone else.

Nadja read a lot, and was fascinated by how the human mind works. She longed to study psychology, but was told that this was not possible. The disability insurance wouldn't support her through such long studies. Nadja would have to do what other disabled people do in Switzerland; take a job as an administrator. Nadja gave in, and completed an apprenticeship with a bank. She has worked at a bank ever since, showing employers everywhere that integrating people with disabilities into the workplace doesn't have to be complicated.

Nadja's mental health is very strong. Her way of seeing the world inspires others. She visits schools, answers all the children's questions, and helps them understand that she is just like them, in spite of living with a disability.

When Nadja was seventeen, her brother died. Nadja reacted by deciding to live her life to the full, and to move forward with even more happiness and joy. First, she got a tattoo. This was her way of saying: 'Hey, look at me, people. I'm a person, too!'

She got more tattoos, grew dreadlocks and even travelled to Thailand with her boyfriend. Now, in her thirties, Nadja likes to party at the bar Goa Nights, and she employs a team of assistants to support her in her own home.

Over the years, Nadja realised that her own happiness is contagious. She found herself helping her assistants to change the way that they thought, changing their lives for the better. So Nadja built on this talent, and her interest in psychology, to set up her own business as a life coach.

Nadja firmly believes that joy can multiply and grow. She sees herself sowing small seeds of joy all around her, changing people's lives, one seed at a time.

'We have to think anyway. Why not be optimistic from the start?'

Elisabeth Kübler-Ross

The Woman Who Spent Her Life Caring for the Dying

1926–2004

During the 1950s, Elisabeth Kübler-Ross – a Swiss physician working in the United States – was shocked that doctors and nurses weren't talking about death with their dying patients! Death was so taboo that doctors even avoided telling patients they were dying. Instead, they told family members, letting them decide whether to tell the patient ... as if the patient's feelings about dying didn't matter.

Back in Switzerland, death was understood to be part of life. Most people died at home, cared for by their friends and family until the end.

Elisabeth Kübler was born in Zurich, the smallest and weakest of triplet sisters, but that didn't hold her back. Naturally protective of the weak or less fortunate, she dreamt of becoming a doctor and caring for people. Her father said she was 'too fragile' for medical school, expecting her to work as a secretary at his office supply company. Elisabeth refused and left home at sixteen, working as a housemaid, then in a chemical lab and finally volunteering at hospitals all over Europe following the Second World War.

When Elisabeth returned to Switzerland, she studied medicine at the prestigious University of Zurich. While there, she fell for a classmate, Emanuel Ross. After getting married, they were working at hospitals in New York when she first noticed how dying patients there were treated.

Elisabeth decided to find a way to change this taboo. She specialised in psychiatry and made it her life's work to educate people about the process of dying. She gave seminars where dying patients came on stage to talk about their feelings. At first, few doctors attended, thinking that it was cruel to ask patients to discuss their own deaths – even though Elisabeth knew the patients actually wanted to talk about it.

Elisabeth went on to write over twenty books about life, death, dying and grief. She named the 'five stages of dealing with death', including Denial, Anger, Bargaining, Depression and Acceptance. Doctors loved this part of her work because they could use it as a tool to label their patients. That frustrated Elisabeth immensely, as plopping a patient into a defined stage was not the point! It was about understanding what dying patients were feeling. Even so, Elisabeth knew that her stages gave doctors and patients an easier way to talk about death.

Elisabeth also started the first hospice programs in the United States, which allow people who are dying to spend their last days at home while getting the medical care they need. Since then, over 4,000 hospice programs have sprung up, every one of them based on Elisabeth's ground-breaking work – and all helping to remove the taboo surrounding death.

'The more you learn, the harder the lessons get.'

Petra Sprecher

The Woman Who Flirts With Danger

Born 1973

On her first job as a stunt woman, Petra Sprecher was strapped into her seat on a makeshift Ferris wheel. Up, up, up she went, when – snap – the axle holding the seat to the wheel broke! This wasn't part of the stunt. This was real. She fell and hit the ground. Hard.

The crew looked on in terror as an ambulance took her away. She was lucky; her injuries were minor. To everyone's surprise, a few weeks later she was back doing stunt work. Petra wanted to be a stunt woman, and nothing was going to stop her.

Even as a child, Petra went after what she wanted. At age seven, she wanted to train with an after-school youth circus in Basel, but her parents couldn't take her. So, Petra travelled alone for an hour, taking both a tram and bus to get there. She ended up training with that circus for ten years.

At twenty, Petra was one of only seven people from around the world admitted to the national circus school in Montreal, Canada. She specialised in 'cloud swing', a dangerous aerial act that involved flips, drops and twists on a rope swing, high in the air. She was so good that she was invited to tour with the amazing Cirque du Soleil.

One of those tour stops brought her to California, USA. She fell in love with Hollywood and wanted to go back. A few months later, while paging through a magazine, she saw an article about African American stunt women in Hollywood. Petra felt the world stop for a second. This was what she wanted to do next!

Petra didn't have connections or experience in Hollywood, but the circus had given her the expertise needed for stunts. Her big break came in 2001, when she was hired to work in the major motion picture *Minority Report*. Despite her fall, she continued doing stunts. Since then, she's worked in numerous movies and TV shows, yet you rarely see her face – while stunt performers face the danger, it's movie stars who face the camera.

Petra has crashed through glass ceilings, jumped off balconies and been sucked into quicksand. In 2016, she was set to get hit by a car – one of the most perilous stunts out there – and for the first time, she thought, 'What am I doing?' Her bag was already packed, just in case her next ride was in an ambulance! Petra did the car-hit, but since then she has no longer been interested in taking such huge risks.

Petra always knows what she wants, and now she wants a change. She's ready to move out of the shadows and into the spotlight again. No doubt she will. For Petra, there is no 'I can't do that'.

'Allow yourself to dream big.'

Susanne Bickel

The Woman Who Became a Famous Egyptologist

Born 1960

Susanne was nine when she first read about the Egyptian Pharaoh Tutankhamen. The story of archeologists discovering his 3,300-year-old tomb awakened a passion to learn more. By the time she was sixteen, Susanne had read everything she could find about ancient Egypt.

When her family moved to from Bern to London for six months, it was a dream come true. Every day, Susanne explored the British Museum's vast Egyptian collection. Towering above her as big as a bus, the sculpture of Pharaoh Ramesses II made her heart pound. Everywhere she looked, ancient Egyptian treasures, mummies, coffins, furniture and jewelry were on display. Each object was covered in symbols called hieroglyphs. Determined to read the stories and letters written over 3,000 years ago, Susanne taught herself at the age of sixteen to read hieroglyphs.

Susanne wanted to study Egyptology at university, but jobs in the field were rare. In fact, at the time, there were only two female Egyptology professors in the world. Luckily, her Greek language teacher encouraged her to follow her passion. He even convinced her parents that she'd learn many skills that are useful in any job, such as languages, problem-solving and the ability to understand other cultures.

But at university, Susanne started to have doubts. Although she loved learning about ancient Egypt, she couldn't see how studying Egyptology helped modern society. A trip to Egypt changed her mind when she saw how the past was woven into the modern people's daily lives. She realised to understand the present, you have to understand what came before. Everybody leaves behind clues to how they lived their lives. As an Egyptologist, Susanne would look for these clues, putting them together like a puzzle, to help tell stories that have been forgotten. She devoted her life to uncovering and sharing the secrets of ancient Egypt.

In 2012, as a professor of Egyptology at the University of Basel, Susanne was on site, leading the excavation of several tombs in the Valley of the Kings – the area where Tutankhamen was found. Susanne and her team discovered the tomb of a priestess named Nehemesbastet. It was the first tomb to be found undisturbed in nearly 100 years!

Susanne's team also dug up a 3,500-year-old sock — the oldest ever found— along with mummified remains of over twenty previously unknown princesses and princes. Sifting through a pile of rubble outside the tombs, Susanne's team also discovered the oldest sundial ever found, proving that it was the Egyptians, not the Greeks, who invented vertical sundials.

Tutankhamen had sparked Susan's desire to learn everything she could about ancient Egypt. Now, over fifty years later, she works close to where his tomb was found, searching for clues to how people lived thousands of years ago.

'Do what you love, and then try to make the practical things in life just work.'

Charlotte Blattner

The Woman Who Protects Animals

Born 1987

Charlotte Blattner was shocked by what she learned about intensive animal farming. Animals, such as chickens or pigs, were being raised on huge farms and jammed in together in tight cages in hot, closed spaces. That alone was horrible. Then she found out that many workers on those farms were forced to live under similar conditions. Sometimes the workers weren't even allowed to take bathroom breaks. Instead, they had to wear diapers all day!

Growing up in Basel-Landschaft, Charlotte was always passionate about two things – justice and animals. She studied law and volunteered at animal shelters and sanctuaries that protected animals, caring for them after abuse and mistreatment. At first, she thought of her passions as separate things. But then she discovered that she could combine them both by working as an animal rights lawyer.

It was during her studies that Charlotte discovered how both animals and workers were treated on huge animal farms all over the world. Their treatment was upsetting, but considering the work Charlotte had already done with animal sanctuaries, not surprising. Charlotte learned that the way people treat animals often mirrors how they treat other people. Intensive animal farming was a perfect example of how companies that who have no respect for animal rights often have no respect for human rights either.

Charlotte was shocked that companies got away with this kind of abuse – even more that these practices are legal. She learned that when governments tried to pass laws protecting the animals and the workers, the companies would just move their farms to other countries to get around the rules. Charlotte decided to find a way to change that.

Charlotte knew that, usually, a government can only apply its laws inside its own country. But there is an exception to this rule when protecting human rights. This is called extraterritorial jurisdiction. If someone is from one country, but is living in another, and they do something that would be illegal in their home country (such as hurting other people or using violence), they could still be prosecuted by the rules of their home country. Charlotte wondered if extraterritorial jurisdiction could protect animals, too.

Charlotte did extensive research on extraterritorial jurisdiction and how it could be applied to animals. This work won her the Marie Heim-Vögtlin Prize in 2020 – a prize given by the Swiss National Science Foundation to outstanding woman researchers. Charlotte hopes that this honour will give her project exposure and that it will be put into practice to protect animals and workers around the world.

This is just the start for Charlotte. Going forward, she wants to show how the law can be used to reverse climate change, protect biodiversity and prove that in this world everyone – and every being – deserves to be protected.

'If you are passionate about something, you have the power to create that job yourself.'

Germaine de Staël

The Woman Who Took on Napoleon Bonaparte

1766–1817

In 1811, Germaine de Staël pretended to go out for a little stroll. She stepped out of her castle in Coppet (near Geneva), past Napoleon's soldiers, and into her horse-drawn carriage. She wasn't going for a stroll, though. She was off on a secret escape to England. Hidden away in her carriage was the manuscript of a book. With this journey, Germaine was defying the most powerful man of her time: Napoleon Bonaparte, the mighty French emperor.

Growing up in Paris to Swiss parents, Germaine loved politics, but she soon understood that as a woman, she could never become a politician herself. But she learned how to sway minds with her knowledge and sharp wit. She threw the best parties in all of Paris. She invited the most powerful Parisians to these parties, called 'salons'. They would gather and discuss new ideas, and whenever Germaine spoke, everybody listened.

When Napoleon Bonaparte rose to power, Germaine was delighted at first. Here was a man who would help France finally become a democratic country – a country in which the people had a say! However, she soon saw that Napoleon was acting more like a dictator, grabbing power for himself instead of giving it to the people.

When Germaine turned against Napoleon, her friends listened. They also turned against him. Napoleon grew afraid of Germaine's power.

'They say that she does not speak of politics or me; but how does it happen that all who speak to her come to like me less?' he asked a friend.

Napoleon banned Germaine from Paris, ordered her back to her castle in Coppet, forbade her to leave the house and placed his agents all around her. He had her books burnt. But Germaine de Staël would not be silenced! She invited Napoleon's enemies to her salons in Coppet, and kept writing passionate letters and books.

When Germaine was ready to publish *On Germany,* a book promoting democracy, she was not going to let anyone stop her. Not even Napoleon himself. So, she set out in her horse-drawn carriage. Napoleon's troops were everywhere. To avoid them, Germaine criss-crossed Europe, travelling via Austria, Russia and Sweden on her mission to get the manuscript to England where it could be published.

In 1814, one of her contemporaries wrote 'There are three great powers struggling against Napoleon for the soul of Europe: England, Russia and Madame de Staël.'

In 1815, Napoleon was defeated and exiled from France. Germaine could at last return to her beloved Paris.

'The greatest happiness is to transform one's feelings into action.'

Jacqueline Urbach

The Woman Who Is a True Visionary

Date of Birth: Top Secret

In 1966, Jacqueline Urbach, a young optician from Switzerland, was working in Los Angeles when she saw something remarkable that changed the course of her life. It was another woman's eyes. Brown eyes that sparkled and shone just like the Hollywood stars Jacqueline had admired as a child in Zurich.

Looking closer, Jacqueline realised that the irises of the woman's eyes were naturally flecked with gold. How incredible it would be to add golden flecks to eyes that didn't have them naturally! But how? Jacqueline, like all other opticians back then, only had experience producing eyeglasses and clear, hard contact lenses. That's when it dawned on her – she could invent contact lenses with golden flecks imbedded into them. That way, everyone who wore them could sparkle like a Hollywood star.

By that time in her life, Jacqueline knew that some things didn't come easy. She'd struggled in school where several teachers told her that she would never amount to anything. She nearly quit school, but then one teacher made all the difference. He told her that she could accomplish anything she set her mind to. Inspired by his faith in her, she went from the worst student to the best in her class within one year. It was hard work. But she would not quit.

After she saw the woman's eyes, Jacqueline started experimenting with colour. At first, she painted the insides of the hard lenses and etched details into them. But that looked artificial. Then inspiration struck. She could add glitter to the insides of the lenses! She bought gold glitter at a toy store and got to work. After months of trial and error, she found a way to embed the glitter between two acrylic layers in the lenses.

The major movie studios heard about Jacqueline's invention and started ordering lenses for movie stars to wear. Jacqueline knew that she had invented something extraordinary. She patented her idea.

About this same time, another company developed the first soft contact lenses. Jacqueline knew that soft lenses would be more comfortable to wear than hard ones … and more popular. So, she put her colourful hard lenses aside, bought new equipment and started teaching herself to make soft lenses.

It took years of effort, but she did it, and even improved the design of soft contact lenses. Jacqueline's six patents changed the way that both hard and soft, and clear and coloured, contact lenses are made all over the world.

'I consider my work as my hobby; thinking and creativity are my nourishment.'

Elisabeth Baulacre

The Woman Who Built an Empire

1613–1693

In 1641, Elisabeth Baulacre's husband died. She was a single mother left alone with a toddler and a small haberdashery business selling items like gloves, bonnets and ribbons. Society expected Elisabeth to either remarry quickly and hand the business over to her new husband or continue with the haberdashery as it was until her son could take over. Elisabeth did neither. She stayed single for years, completely transforming the haberdashery into one of Geneva's most profitable businesses and she ran it herself.

At the time, the simple, plain fashions in many parts of Europe were beginning to make way for fancier ones with gold and silver embroidery or embellishments. Elisabeth decided to specialise in production of gold and silver thread. Making this kind of thread was complex and expensive. Each step in the process – melting, stretching and beating gold into fine strips, then winding it around a silken core – required working with different artisans. And those artisans required gold and silver reserves, as well as specific tools. Aspiring workers couldn't even start off in the trade without these materials, and often they didn't have the money to buy them. Elisabeth did.

This is where Elisabeth did things differently than her peers. Instead of hiring artisans on a task by task basis, she gave them money for materials, loaned students the fees needed to become apprentices, supplied housing to workers and even lent money to those in difficulty.

But her loans came with a contract stating they could work only for her until the debts (and interest!) were paid off. Many of Elisabeth's workers were bound to her for ten, twenty years or even longer. She ended up employing over a thousand skilled craftspeople, growing her small business into a massive empire and crushing the competition.

Elisabeth exported her thread all over Europe. She negotiated with merchants in places as far as Amsterdam and London, as well as with local merchants who sent their goods abroad. In 1655, she married a politician and her influence also extended to politics. People even said that if someone wanted to get elected in Geneva, it was almost impossible to do so without Elisabeth's support! After fifty years of expanding her empire and 'buying' her employees' loyalty, Elisabeth Baulacre died as the second richest person in Geneva.

Did Elisabeth have a heart of gold? Probably not. But thanks to her savvy, she did have an enterprise full of it.

Margrit Rusterholz

The Woman Who Loves To Go Fast

Born 1942

Everyone stared at the only woman in the race. Dressed head to toe in black leather, Margrit tugged the old fighter-pilot goggles down from her helmet to protect her eyes. Crouched low over her motorcycle, she revved its engine, hit the gas and shot up the hill like a rocket.

In 1942, near Zurich, the Reiser family was expecting a baby boy. Instead, Margrit arrived and was named after the midwife! Even though her mother insisted she 'behave like a girl', Margrit preferred to climb trees, build miniature cities out of Mecanno kits and play with her model train set. Dolls weren't her thing.

Margrit's first motorcycle ride was as a passenger on the back of her boyfriend Fritz's bike. She loved the speed, so Fritz encouraged her to learn to drive a motorcycle and to start competing in Swiss hill climb races. But her parents stopped her – girls definitely didn't ride motorcycles. When Fritz died in a crash, Margrit repaired his damaged motorcycle by herself and, ignoring her parents, started to practice racing.

A year later, Margrit zipped along twisty alpine roads, testing how fast she could go. In 1962, at the age of twenty, she was the first woman to compete in the Swiss hill climb championship in Villars sur Ollon. By 1963, she beat 80% of the other racers in the 125 ccm class – and was still the only woman racing! She also became a part of the East German national team and competed in races on a national level.

At the time, the motorcycle racing rules favoured men. Back then, motorcycles were started by the rider placing their heel onto a lever and kicking it downwards. Because timekeeping began with the first kick to start the engine, a heavier and stronger rider had an advantage. So, Margrit asked the National Motorcycling Federation to change the rules. Against the odds, they changed the rule so that the race started with a running engine. That levelled the playing field.

Margit got a lot of attention for being the only woman on a motorcycle. She was pulled over by the police so often, she says, 'If there had been an award for getting stopped by the police, I'd have won it!' So, Margrit rode with her hair loose, a long flowing skirt and high heels to shock them even more.

All her life, she'd been told to slow down, to be more lady-like. But Margrit never let other people's expectations of what women could or should do stop her. After starting a family, Margrit switched to riding fast horses. With her husband Bruno, she started a breeding farm for Icelandic horses, competed in races and taught generations of kids to ride.

'If you can't go fast, why bother?'

08
21
21

Tilo Frey

The Woman Who Broke Barriers

1923–2008

In Neuchâtel, there was once a square that was named after a scientist who tried to prove that white people were superior to people of colour. Different groups around the world followed his racist theories leading to death and pain for many people. But today, that square is named after someone else. Today, that square is named after Tilo Frey.

Tilo's father was Swiss and her mother was from Cameroon. She moved with her father to Neuchâtel when she was five, and Tilo immediately noticed that she was different. People called her names like *'la négresse'*, a hateful term that taunted her for being black, and even suggested that she was less than human. Tilo's father wanted her to be safe and fit in as much as possible. He advised her to 'act as white as a lily', meaning that she should act like the people around her – who were mostly white.

Tilo was always very driven. When she finished her studies, she taught business classes and was even the director of the *École Professionnelle des Jeunes Filles.* But she was also interested in politics. She was the first woman of colour elected to the Neuchâtel Grand Council in 1969. In 1971, she decided to run for a seat in the National Council. That was unheard of! A mixed-race woman running for one of the highest seats in the country? Her proposal was clear. If elected, she would push for women's rights, but she would also help Switzerland build closer relationships with other countries – in particular, developing countries.

Unfortunately, the newspapers and TV reporters didn't care about her proposals. Instead, they criticised her because of who she was. She had dark skin. She wasn't married. She was ambitious. It scared them.

Tilo was so certain she was going to lose the election that she went home early on election night. She didn't even bother to stick around to hear the results. But much to everyone's surprise, she did win, and was among the first group of women to ever be elected to the National Council.

Traditionally, members of the National Council were recommended to wear dark colours in the parliamentary sessions. But for once, Tilo wanted to be white as a lily—not to fit in, but to stick out. Tilo Frey wore white. She was one of the first women to be elected to the National Council, and the first person of African descent. She was proud of who she was, and she would wear what she wanted. And now, in changing the square to *Espace Tilo Frey*, the city of Neuchâtel has shown that it is proud of her as well.

'Women have to do twice as much and then smile.'

Sophie Täuber-Arp

The Woman Who Made Art Against War

1889–1943

'If you continue this dangerous Dada nonsense, we will have to fire you,' said the director of the School of Applied Arts in Zurich. Sophie Täuber-Arp couldn't afford to be fired. She needed her income as a teacher. And yet, she could not, and would not, stop creating the art she felt compelled to make!

Sophie grew up in Trogen, in eastern Switzerland. This was an area where many people earned part of their living from weaving cloth on their weaving looms at home. Sophie loved being surrounded by people working with patterns and shapes, but most people at the time didn't think that working with textiles was proper art. They thought that the only art that counted was fine art painting.

Sophie disagreed, so she studied both fine art and textile design. But even that wasn't enough for her. Sophie wanted to experiment with many different art forms, play with all materials. She moved to Munich, Germany where she learned woodwork, made sculptures, studied architecture and practiced dance.

Sophie's art is full of life: in her paintings, shapes are delicately balanced, and dots look as if they were dancing. Her sculptures are elegant and often practical (such as her famous wooden powder compacts).

In 1914, the First World War broke out. Sophie returned from Germany back to neutral Switzerland and settled in Zurich. Soon, thousands of refugees escaped the war to the safety of Switzerland. Among them were famous artists from all over Europe. Zurich became a hotbed of arts and culture, and Sophie was right in the middle of it all.

Sophie and her friends watched powerless as the war ravaged through Europe. This mad war was killing millions of people. It made no sense! They responded with a wild howl of creation. Just like the world made no sense, their art became deliberately nonsensical. A new art form was born – Dadaism.

Because it was so new, strange and different, most people viewed Dadaism as stupid, useless and even dangerous. When the school where Sophie was teaching found out about her involvement with the Dadaists, they threatened to fire her. Teaching was Sophie's main income. She couldn't risk losing her job. So, she continued creating Dadaist art in secret. Pretending to be somebody else, she created fantastical marionettes, designed costumes for performances, sculpted masks, painted sets for plays and danced to experimental poetry.

By 1928, Sophie had made a name for herself, and could live off her art. She resigned from her teaching job, and finally felt free to reveal the art that she had created, and who she really was. Today, Sophie Täuber-Arp is recognised as one of the ground-breaking artists of the 20th century.

'It is gaiety, basically, that allows us to have no fear before the problems of life and to find a natural solution to them.'

Margrit Läubli

The Woman for Whom Life Is a Cabaret

Born 1928

Margrit Läubli stood on the Cabaret Cornichon stage, wondering what to do. She knew that cabaret involved singing, dancing and comedy skits in front of a live audience. But how to audition, exactly? No idea! She was handed a funny script to read and was asked to sing a song. She chose *'Ruf zu mein Vaterland'*, the boring Swiss national anthem. She did well, apparently. Moments later, she was hired.

As a young girl, Margrit dreamt of becoming a ballet dancer. At sixteen, Margrit's mother agreed that she could spend the 20Fr she was earning monthly as a dressmaker's apprentice to pay for ballet lessons. Margrit ran to sign up at the Stadttheater Zürich, where she was told that the fee had increased to 25Fr. She couldn't afford it! Instead of leaving defeated, young Margrit demanded to speak with the director. Impressed by her audacity, he invited her to audition so he could see her dance. She'd never taken a ballet class, so she improvised, moving her body as she thought a ballet dancer should. The director said she had natural talent and helped her find a scholarship that paid for her ballet lessons in full.

Margrit danced for the next five years in both Zurich and Paris. She loved it, but she also longed to perform as a solo artist, and to somehow combine dance with the spoken word. One of the ballet choreographers mentioned that Cabaret Cornichon was looking for new performers. Cabaret was the perfect fit! It allowed performers to poke fun at the serious topics of the time, turning them into something lighter. Margrit knew laughter was a wonderful medicine ... and she wanted to spread it around.

A few years later, Margrit met César Keiser, another talented cabaret artist, while working at the Cabaret Fédéral. It was love at first sight. Shortly afterwards, they left Cabaret Fédéral, developed their own two-person show, delighting audiences and making people laugh for the next forty-five years.

After one of their shows, the two were laughing late into the night when there was a knock at the door. Neighbours had complained about noise, so two policemen were sent to the house. But the two officers were so entertained, they stopped and listened under Margrit and César's window before knocking. They asked the two comedians to continue joking around – but to close their windows first.

After César passed away in 2007, Margrit decided that their show must go on. To this day, she still performs their scripts, reading for both roles and giving people the gift of laughter through good times and bad.

'I don't want a problem-free life, but one that is interesting.'

Josephine Clofullia

The Woman Who Had a Beard

1831–1870

In July of 1853, William Chaar paid his twenty-five-cent entrance fee to P. T. Barnum's American Museum, only to storm out in fury. He sued the museum, arguing that Madame Josephine Clofullia, the famous Swiss Bearded Lady, was not a lady at all, but a man in a dress. Yet several witness statements, including three doctors' certificates, declared that Josephine was indeed a woman. Just a very hairy one.

When Josephine Boisdechêne was born in Versoix, a thin, downy layer of hair covered her skin. Her parents weren't worried until, already at age two, some of that down became an actual beard! Doctors were baffled. The only advice they could offer was to never shave the girl's whiskers, for fear they would come in even thicker. So, Josephine's beard grew. Despite this, she was brought up just like other middle-class girls: she was taught how to be a lady. In school, she excelled at needlework and etiquette and poise. Her schoolmates and neighbours got used to the extra hair on her face and, in the end, didn't make much of it.

But for those who didn't know her, Josephine was a curiosity. By the time she was a teenager, her beard was full, dark and over fifteen centimetres long. She lived directly across from Versoix's fancy Hotel du Lac and was often seen by hotel guests. Word spread, and soon Josephine was offered jobs in theatre and sideshow tours. Her father refused the offers, until one day the money was too good to turn down. Josephine and her father set off with a Lyon theatre company and toured all over France. She wore feminine dresses of ruffles and lace, and styled her beard into a point like Napoleon III, the Emperor of France. It's rumoured that Napoleon III was so flattered by this, he gave her a large diamond – which she wore in her beard.

Josephine married and toured Europe under the name *Madame Clofullia*. She gave birth to a little boy … who also had a beard! Invited to New York, she became part of a show in P. T. Barnum's American Museum. There, Josephine was on display with her infant son along with others such as a giantess, an albino lady and the smallest woman alive. To bring attention to the show, P. T. Barnum had William Chaar go to the museum, claim the Swiss Bearded Lady was really a man and sue! This publicity stunt worked like a charm. Over the next few years, well over three million people paid to see Josephine Clofullia in America alone. She ended up touring the world and becoming one of the most famous bearded ladies ever.

'Josephine Clofullia is a perfect lady in every aspect.'
– from the *New Albany Daily Ledger*, 1854

Simone Schwegler

The Woman Who Blazed a Trail as an Improv Actress

Born 1984

The entire audience was roaring with laughter. Sitting near the front row, Simone soon had tears streaming down her face as she watched the actors spontaneously invent characters and scenes – without a script! She'd never seen improv before, and it was love at first sight.

When she was a teenager in Zurich, Simone loved to create and perform stories as a girl scout leader, but being a professional actress had never crossed her mind. She didn't really know what she wanted to do, but it had to be creative and involve people. So, she tried lots of things, like working on a farm with mentally disabled people and even joining a circus in Costa Rica.

That night she saw her first improv performance in 2005, everything changed. Unlike classical theatre, improv actors invent characters, scenes and stories right on the stage, sometimes involving the audience. Simone loved the actors' creativity, spontaneity and the way they built on each other's ideas.

When Simone rushed home and googled 'Improv', she found a course on Tuesday nights. But this was the same night her amateur theatre group met. She expected they'd be mad at her for leaving. So, she was completely surprised when the whole group signed up for the course and dove into this new style of theatre together.

Back then, improv wasn't well known in Switzerland. Everyone thought improv artists were just too lazy to learn the script. There were no female role models and it was impossible to make a living. But Simone was determined to find a way to make improv her career.

For a few years Simone worked part-time as a primary school teacher to pay the bills while she performed improv. But when the primary school hired someone else, she was out of a job. At first Simone was devastated, then her friend Gerry encouraged her to follow her dream. Simone left for Chicago and then Calgary with seven friends to study and perform with some of the pioneers in improv.

After two years of performing and teaching improv with Gerry across Europe, Simone joined *anundpfirsich*, Switzerland's first professional improv troupe. They found theatre space to perform and teach improv classes. Now Simone even teaches improv skills such as collaboration and flexibility to help businesspeople succeed. As the co-owner and former artistic director of *anundpfirsich*, Simone's ideas and performances have helped improv grow in popularity and inspired other women to become professional improv actresses.

Now Simone loves nothing more than when an entire audience laughs at her. Whether it's imaginary egg yolk running down her face or flying through the air like superwoman or simply a ridiculous misunderstanding. That's great improv, and that is what she does.

'Play is the highest form of research' – Albert Einstein

Clotilde Bressler-Gianoli

The Woman Who Loved to Sing

ca. 1875–1912

NEW YORK, 1907. Clotilde Bressler-Gianoli was performing *Carmen* at the Manhattan Opera House when she felt the prick of a knife in her arm. The knife was supposed to be a prop knife, and so not very sharp. But someone had made a mistake, and when her co-star used the real knife on stage, it cut into her! But that wasn't going to stop Clotilde.

Growing up in Geneva, Clotilde's entire family were artists. Her father was a decorator, and her brothers were sculptors and painters. She started playing the piano when she was four, holding her first public concert at the age of seven. Even though Clotilde won many awards while still young, she quickly realised her true love was singing, and at sixteen she studied opera in Geneva and Milan.

Clotilde had a voice that wasn't typical for the opera. She had a tremendous range, so she could sing notes from very low to very high. She used that talent to weave a very special kind of operatic magic when she sang. She also had an amazing stage presence. When she performed, the audience couldn't take their eyes off her. She was like a magnet. She took the audience on an operatic adventure ... and they loved her for it.

Clotilde became an international opera star. After her first concert in Geneva, she performed in major cities like London, Lyon, New York, Marseille, Brussels, San Francisco and Milan. She performed some of the most iconic roles in opera and made them her own. Even after she was stabbed in the arm in New York, she returned to performing the very next night. Despite her massive success, she had to choose between a career on the road, constantly travelling during the season, and having a stable home life. In the end she chose to go home, marry, and have a family. That didn't mean she gave up music though! She was still a star of the stage, singing in the operas that she loved. Her son Henri even joined her in New York for a while, when she was performing there. It was important to her that she could choose when she sang, and where. She also taught at the Conservatory in Lausanne, where she shared her passion and talent for music with her students.

At the time of her death in 1912, Clotilde was many things: a singer, a performer, a teacher, a mother, a wife. Her entire life was shaped by a passion for music and a love of performing – and not even an accidental stabbing was going to slow her down.

'Her portrayal as Carmen has: "the allurement of sheer wickedness and all the wiles and treacheries that wickedness suggests".'
– *The New York Times*, 15 December 1906

TIME TO ACT
SAVE OUR ONLY HOME
ACTION NOW!
TIME IS RUNNING OUT
THERE IS NO PLANET B
CLIMATE JUSTICE NOW!
SYSTEM CHANGE NOT CLIMATE CHANGE
WHAT I STAND FOR IS WHAT I STAND ON
STRIKE for CLIMATE

Marie-Claire Graf

The Woman Who Fights for Climate Justice

Born 1996

When Marie-Claire Graf first visited the Morteratsch Glacier as a child, she imagined a huge, mighty white beast on the mountainside. She was disappointed. What she saw was a sad, grey, shrivelled-up slab of ice. Marie-Claire learned that over the past hundred years, the glacier had shrunk by over two kilometres and that, year by year, it was shrinking even further. Soon there might be nothing left of one of the longest glaciers in eastern Switzerland. This was the first time that Marie-Claire came face to face with the changes global warming is bringing to the world.

Growing up, Marie-Claire was inspired by people like Bruno Manser, who fought to save the rainforest and its people, and Ursula Brunner, who fought to establish fair trade in Switzerland. Marie-Claire wanted to fight against climate change, but she wasn't sure how. The people around her didn't seem to worry much about the subject. Marie-Claire felt lonely and frustrated.

This changed when Marie-Claire moved to Zurich for her studies. Suddenly, she met lots of people who wanted to take action for the climate. At their university, they set up a 'Sustainability Week', organising a week's worth of workshops about subjects ranging from turtles and plastic pollution to vegan cookery classes. At the end of the week they served a huge 'zero waste' buffet meal. The buffet was leftover food collected from nearby restaurants in just one evening – food that otherwise would all have been thrown away.

The week was a huge success. Students at different universities around the world took up the idea, and have now organised their own Sustainability Weeks.

Marie-Claire attended international climate conferences, but she was still only twenty-two years old. Many people didn't take her seriously. How could she make young people's voices heard? Then, in early December 2018, Marie-Claire met Greta Thunberg at a conference. Six months earlier, Greta had been just a Swedish teenager striking by herself in front of the Swedish parliament. Now she had spoken at the UN and was famous around the world.

'Why don't you just strike?' Greta suggested. Marie-Claire decided to give it a go. She started a 'school strike' group on her phone. Within hours, hundreds of people had joined the group, and a couple of weeks later, the first school strike took place in Zurich. Marie-Claire knew now that lots of people cared, and wanted change. It was just a question of bringing everyone together. So that's what she did.

In September 2019, six million children worldwide took to the streets, demanding that governments take action on the Climate Crisis. 100,000 people marched in Switzerland alone. Leading the way, Marie-Claire Graf.

'We already have all the solutions to stop the climate crisis. All we now need is courage and determination.'

Marthe Gosteli

The Woman Who Saved the History of Swiss Women

1917–2017

Marthe Gosteli's father died when she was forty years old, leaving Marthe, her sister and her mother to run the family farm in Worblaufen, Bern. The only problem was – it was 1957. Even though the three women were intelligent adults, they had no right to keep their home without the consent of a man.

When Marthe was growing up, girls were expected to learn knitting, sewing and cooking, while the boys studied history, science and geometry. Girls didn't need maths if they were going to grow up to be mothers and homemakers!

Back then, Swiss women weren't allowed to vote. Marthe's parents, both interested in politics, thought that women should have a voice in government. When Marthe was eleven, they took her to the 1928 Swiss Exhibition for Women's Work parade in Bern. One of the parade floats displayed a giant model snail, representing women's frustration with how slowly the government was reacting to their demand to vote.

In 1949, Marthe joined the Bernese Women's Suffrage Association (ASF), a group fighting for women's voting rights. She also worked for the American Embassy and was impressed that American women had won the right to vote in 1920. There was even a female US ambassador to Switzerland! It was the first time Marthe had met a woman in a real position of power.

In 1957, when Marthe's father died and the family farm was very nearly taken away, a male friend had to step in to help them. Marthe knew it was time to enter the fight for women's rights. She joined the Federation of Swiss Women's Associations (BSF), leading the group dedicated to political rights for women.

Marthe reached out to people in quiet ways: she created pamphlets and went door-to-door to talk about women's right to vote. She encouraged women to approach their village or town offices to ask about voting, and to get involved in their local governments. She had women talk to the men in their lives, encouraging them to pin green ribbons on their jackets to show their support of women's rights. Eventually, these quiet tactics worked!

On 7 February 1971, two-thirds of Swiss men voted that women should have the right to vote. It brought attention to the other urgent issues affecting women: getting the right to manage their own bank accounts, earning equal pay, owning property and getting paid maternity leave.

And even after this victory, Marthe didn't want the history of the Swiss women's suffrage movement to get lost. She knew that the male-dominated government weren't likely to collect and archive the important documents, posters, photos and stories. So, Marthe donated the Gosteli family home and started filling it with historical items. You can still visit the Gosteli Foundation today and learn about all the brave Swiss women who fought so long for their right to vote.

'They called me a suffragette. And that wasn't meant nicely.'

Rocio Restrepo

The Woman Who Made a Place for Herself

Born 1961

From 2005–2007, Rocio Restrepo took her notebook and pen with her wherever she went in Geneva, ready to talk to strangers. Hearing women speak with a foreign accent or in a foreign language sparked Rocio into action. In the supermarket, at the park, on the street – Rocio approached these women, introduced herself and started asking questions. The answers she got confirmed that what she had suspected was true. Now ... what would she do about it?

In 1999, Rocio had had to leave her home in Colombia. The country had been in a civil war for decades, and though Rocio had a successful life there it became too dangerous to stay. She, her husband and her children came to Geneva as refugees.

Rocio was thankful to be safe. But Geneva was scary for other reasons: everything was different there. Rocio knew no one. She didn't speak French. The people in Geneva didn't pinch babies' cheeks or holler to each other across the street. Even the way those streets were laid out was different, with names instead of only numbers. Rocio had to re-learn everything. She felt like a newborn baby, not a thirty-eight-year-old woman!

In Colombia, Rocio had worked as a businesswoman. But in Switzerland, her diplomas and eighteen years of work experience weren't accepted. Rocio applied for over 200 jobs. No matter how hard she tried, no one would hire her. Despite having studied and excelled in her field for most of her life, she ended up having to clean houses and babysit children.

Rocio was sad. She lost confidence. But she had to know – was it just her, or were other immigrant women also having the same problems?

She got out her notebook and pen and started a survey. She talked to immigrant women all over Geneva, asking about their education and experience, then comparing that to their current job in Switzerland. The results were overwhelming: skilled immigrant women were not hired for jobs that that they were trained to do! Instead they worked as nannies or cleaners, and, like Rocio, many were unhappy.

Rocio decided it was time to change this. In 2007, she created an association called *découvrir* ('discover') to help immigrant women create new goals, regain their confidence and find jobs that fit their experience. Every year, *découvir* helps hundreds of women. Not only does it help them, it helps Switzerland, too! Their diverse experiences and knowledge add value to Swiss society.

After arriving in Geneva, it took Rocio a long time to find a way to put her skills to use and to feel happy with whom she'd become. She wants other women to figure it out much more quickly! That's why Rocio helps women like her, and why she insists those women then help others too. Together, they make Switzerland home. For everyone.

'To be supportive and caring makes our existence easier and gives it meaning.'

Maria-Theresia Zwyssig

The Woman Who Trekked the Great Himalayan Trail

Born 1986

Maria-Theresia watched the porters turn away from her. 'What's going on?!' she screamed. Ignoring her, they retreated down the mountain with all of the supplies, quitting after just three weeks. Maria collapsed in the snow, devastated. She couldn't trek the world's highest mountain range alone. She had to turn back.

Growing up in Seelisberg, Maria-Theresia had dreamt of flying a Rega Air-Rescue helicopter. But when it came time to choose an occupation, she couldn't find one she liked. Then a friend suggested Maria-Theresia teach English in Nepal. For three months, she lived in a remote village with the Tsewang family. She felt at home there, and knew she'd return one day.

Five years later, when Maria-Theresia wanted to visit the Tsewang family, she decided to go by bike, alone, from Switzerland. She'd never done anything like it before and wanted to see if she could. It took her nearly a year to pedal the 10,333 kilometres through twenty-two countries along the Silk Road. Along the way, she learned how to keep going when things got tough.

One day she read about Nepal's Great Himalayan Trail (GHT), the world's highest and most difficult trekking route. Only fifty people had completed the 1,711 km long trail, which takes 150 days to trek. To build the strength she'd need to succeed, she biked to Nepal, covering 15,000 kilometres over a full year, visiting Russia, Japan and China on the way. When she arrived in Kathmandu, Nepal's capital city, she had exactly 150 days on her tourist visa to organise and trek the GHT.

After three weeks into the trek, her fingertips cracked and bled from the cold, dry air. But walking in the bitter cold at high altitude wasn't the hardest part. Instead, it was her team. Her guide and porters were ill-prepared and didn't take the trek seriously. When the porters quit, Maria-Theresia had to backtrack down the mountain.

Back in Kathmandu, Maria-Theresia couldn't stop crying. With just ninety days left on her visa, her dream seemed impossible. Luckily, she found Sanjip, a new guide, who had a plan and an experienced team. They would walk for eighty-nine days, fourteen hours and up to twenty kilometres per day. Maria-Theresia wasn't sure she could do it.

But they did. Together they trekked through ice-cold rivers, climbed seventeen 5,000-metre-high mountain passes and walked for nearly 1,000 hours. Sanjip even convinced Maria-Theresia to keep walking while covered in blood-sucking leeches. They fought the bitter cold, high altitude, injury and exhaustion to complete the GHT as a team!

For Maria-Theresia, trekking the GHT was more than an adventure. She learned you can do many things on your own, but with the right people around you, you can do the impossible.

'Only by going beyond your limits, with an open heart, will you achieve your dreams.'

Katharina Samara-Wickrama

The Woman Who Helps Women and Girls Find Their Voice

Born 1963

When Katharina Samara-Wickrama was eight years old, she made an important decision. She was going to be Batman. It made perfect sense – she wanted to help people, and that is what Batman does. All she needed was a superpower.

As she got older, Katharina decided that studying law was a more realistic choice. Her father had told her that in order to make the world a better place, she didn't have to change everything all at once, but make it better for one person at a time. So that's what she tried to do. She worked as a lawyer and volunteered at a women's legal centre, helping women facing different issues like workplace bullying, child custody battles and divorce. But she wanted to do even more, so she went to work for a United Nations agency that helps refugees.

In refugee camps people often live in small, confined spaces. They have to share basic resources, like water and toilets. They're not allowed leave the camps. Many only have what is given to them. Because of this, refugees may feel angry, scared and helpless. Sometimes there is violence in the camps. The camps can be dangerous for women and girls, who are often attacked when going out to get water from streams or firewood from the forest.

Katharina's job was to help those women and girls. But no matter how much she and her team tried to find ways to end the violence, it didn't stop. That's when she realised the problem: no one was actually asking the women themselves what they needed!

For decades, organisations had decided what the refugees got. They might send yoga mats to Haiti after an earthquake, or give refugees food that was so unfamiliar they wouldn't know how to cook it. But the refugees themselves knew best what they needed to make their lives better and safer, and so Katharina was determined that organisations should hear their voices and act on the solutions they suggested.

As Geneva is the world centre of humanitarian work, she knew that this was the place to start. It took Katharina years to find other people who thought like her. Many just didn't see the point: they felt that people should be happy with whatever help they were getting. But eventually, Katharina did find other people who agreed. And they began to change the way these programs worked.

Katharina didn't become Batman or a superhero. But she did realise that we all have a superpower – we can listen to others. By listening, we can make the world better for one person at a time.

'Everything I have is because someone else sacrificed to open those doors for me. I have a sense of responsibility to them to make sure their sacrifice was worth it.'

Ella Maillart

The Woman Who Loved Adventure

1903–1997

When they were children, Ella Maillart and her best friend Hermine de Saussure would play in their boat on Lake Geneva and imagine wild adventures: sailing in the Mediterranean Sea, thrown about by huge waves, discovering new lands they named after the places they had read about: Vladivostok, Alaska, Siberia. But Ella was a sickly child. How could she hope to ever travel far away?

Ella spent long days tucked up in bed, until she discovered that sports helped her feel much better. From that moment on, Ella was unstoppable. She sailed all summer and skied all winter. She set up the first women's field hockey team in Geneva just so she could play. Hermine and Ella won their first sailing races at thirteen, and Ella competed in the 1924 Olympic Games as the only female sailor!

Ella's parents wanted her to learn a profession, to settle down, but Ella had different plans. With Hermine, she intended to sail from Europe all the way to Polynesia. For two years they worked to prepare their boat on the ocean shore in France. However, a few months before leaving, Hermine fell ill. The friends had to abandon their plans. Hermine returned to Geneva, and later got married, leaving Ella alone and stranded.

Ella was heartbroken. She didn't know who she was, where she belonged or what she wanted to do with her life. She did know, however, that she wanted to be outside, feel the wind on her face and the earth beneath her feet. She would never be tied to a house in the city, or stuck to a profession. Against all her family's and friends' advice and expectations, she soon set off again, eastwards this time, to explore Russian Turkestan – one of the most remote regions of the world.

Ella rode on horseback and walked with camel caravans across large, unexplored swathes of Central Asia. She slept in nomads' tents and in shepherds' huts, trekked through China during civil war, climbed steep Himalayan mountain passes, explored Tibet and India. To pay for her trips, Ella wrote newspaper articles and books about her adventures. She photographed and filmed the people she encountered, carrying her heavy equipment with her everywhere. Her archive of films and photographs document ways of life that have all but disappeared. They have become a treasure trove for historians.

Eventually, Ella found a home for herself in the village of Chandolin in Valais, high up in the Swiss mountains, but, right until her death in 1997, she remained full of curiosity and never stopped travelling and exploring.

'Reading is all very well, but it's better to go and see for yourself. After all, the world belongs to me, and I want to see it, want to go into the deserts and the mountains ...'

Anna Weckerin

The Woman Who Dared to Write a Cookbook

ca. 1535–1596

When her husband suggested that she write down her medicinal recipes, Anna Weckerin was worried. Unlike him, she wasn't a physician. Women weren't allowed to become doctors. What if she made mistakes? Would doctors laugh at her?

Not much is known about Anna personally. In the sixteenth century, most writers were men – and men didn't write much about women. Few women were taught to write, but we know that Anna could. In fact, she was one of the few women of her time to have published poetry. In 1586, she published 'Hochzeit Spruch' – a wedding poem – for friends who were getting married.

Anna's husband Johann was the *Stadtarzt* – city doctor – in Basel, and later in Colmar. Anna joined Johann as he visited patients, and she listened to their various health problems. While Johann treated them, Anna suggested foods that might help. Over time, she built up a lot of knowledge about foods and their potential to help prevent and cure diseases. Today, we call this 'dietetics', but in the sixteenth century, this idea was revolutionary!

Back then, the only alternative to a doctor's diagnosis was the advice of an apothecary. Although apothecaries eventually became the pharmacists we know and trust today, they were nothing of the sort back then. They could offer any kind of 'cures' they wanted, such as leeches, or animal urine, blood or ground-up bone for ... well, pretty much anything. Some apothecaries even sold pulverised mummy as a remedy for cough and sore throat! Anna and Johann doubted many of these 'cures', trusting instead in the healing properties of foods.

Anna's knowledge became so vast, and Johann was so impressed, that he asked her to write down her observations. This way, other doctors and their patients could benefit from her experience. Anna worried that the other physicians and scientists would criticise her work, but Johann promised to review her writing and edit wherever needed.

When Johann died in 1586, Anna's book was not yet complete. Several of Johann's colleagues had heard about Anna's work and encouraged her to finish it so they could use her ideas with their own patients. Anna got back to work, completing the book in 1596. Her ideas included an early version of muesli and instructions to wash salad before eating it. She even suggested placing the wet salad in a cloth and whipping it in circles over the head ... the first salad spinner!

Anna's cookbook, *Ein Köstlich new Kochbuch* (An Exquisite New Cookbook) was printed in multiple editions over the next one hundred years, making it one of the most popular cookbooks of its time.

'The sick become happy when they see something out of the ordinary.'

Ruth Dreifuss

The Woman Who Was the First Female Swiss President

Born 1940

Ruth Dreifuss was born into a home full of love, surrounded by a world full of hate.

The Second World War raged. Nazi Germany – led by Adolf Hitler – was massacring Jewish people. Ruth's parents were Jewish and lived in St Gallen, near the German border. Fear sent them westward, first to Bern, then Geneva. When the war ended, Ruth watched her parents drink their 'Hitler Wine' – a bottle they'd set aside only to be opened once Hitler was defeated. At age five, Ruth didn't drink the wine. Yet she could taste the hope that came with it. A hope that the world would now be a better and more equal place.

As a child, Ruth dreamed of becoming an archaeologist or historian. She wanted to understand how ancient societies worked. But as she got older, she decided she'd rather help shape her own society. To make a big impact, Ruth would need to modify laws and policies. That meant a career in government.

She got into government in 1993, on a 'pink wave'. Women around the country demonstrated by the thousands, demanding female representation on the all-male Federal Council – the highest level of government. After a good deal of fighting within parliament and three rounds of votes, Ruth was elected. She headed the Federal Department of Home Affairs, which deals with everything from equality to environment to culture. Among other things, Ruth fought for equal access to high-quality healthcare, for married women to have their own pensions, and for programs to better help drug addicts. Creating change was difficult and slow. But she was making it happen!

On a Federal Council full of men, Ruth didn't try to act like them. Instead, she stayed true to who she was – a strong and compassionate woman. One time, she knitted sweaters with Bruno Manser, a famous environmentalist working to save the rainforest, and gave them to her colleagues to warm their hearts.

Ruth never forgot what brought her to her position. One wall of her office held pictures of the crowds of women who demonstrated in 1993. Whenever Ruth felt uncertain, she looked at the hope in their eyes and it gave her strength.

In 1999, Ruth was the very first woman and the first person of Jewish descent to become President of the Confederation. It was a huge milestone, with celebrations around the country. Ruth knew, however, that there was still a lot to be done. She fought hardest for those that the government often neglected – refugees, immigrants, women, drug addicts, the infirm and the poor.

Ruth retired from the Federal Council in 2002, but she's still working to make the world a place where hope and equality are not bottled up, but flow freely – at every table, every day.

'Democracy suffers when people live in unequal conditions ...'

91

Eva Nidecker

The Woman Who Is Shaping the Future of Fitness

Born 1980

Eva Nidecker stood in the arrival hall at the airport. She almost couldn't believe it, but the classes she offered at Open Ride were so popular that people were flying to Zurich to come to her indoor cycling studio!

From the first time she tried it, Eva was hooked on indoor cycling. It was unlike any other fitness class she had tried. Because the lights were turned off during the class, her other senses were heightened. In the darkness, Eva focused on her body moving to the rhythm of the music – everything else melted away. Cycling to the beat of the music in the dark was exhilarating. She wanted everyone to experience the same thing.

But the classes she was taking only seemed to attract people already into fitness. They were full of fit young women and lacked diversity. That's when Eva got her crazy idea: she would start her own cycling studio with an open atmosphere that welcomed people of all ages, backgrounds and fitness levels. She felt so strongly about her idea that she left her long-time job as a successful radio, television and event host to make it a reality.

As Eva didn't have a background in the fitness industry, she knew she needed help. So, she hired Rebekah Abdeen, a top indoor cycling instructor and DJ from London, as her creative partner. Together they envisioned a whole new way to approach fitness and decided to call it Open Ride.

Growing up in a musical family in Basel, Eva saw how live music performances united audiences. She knew that sound quality made a huge difference to people's experience, so her studio would be the first to have acoustic panels and a high-quality sound system. Fusing culture and fitness, DJs, musicians and breakdancers would give live performances while people cycled. Eva even designed a wild laser light show so riders felt like they were zipping through space in a rocket.

Instead of looking for traditional fitness instructors like other studios, Eva invited performers and dancers to audition. She wanted inspiring, creative people who loved music to the teach her classes. At Open Ride, it's not unusual to see a male ballet dancer, a lawyer or even a fashion model giving an indoor cycling class.

In less than two years, Eva achieved her dream of making indoor cycling accessible to everyday people. Not only that, but she created an entirely new experience that brings people together through the power of music. With the support of her team at Open Ride, she's shaping the future of fitness. People around the world are taking notice and taking part. Eva's crazy idea turned out to be not so crazy after all.

'Nothing ever goes the way you expect. You have to be flexible and adapt without losing sight of your goals.'

Margrith Bigler-Eggenberger

The Woman Who Became the First Female Federal Judge

Born 1933

On the day of her election, Margrith's father came to her with some very shocking news. Someone had got their hands on her application papers for the job of federal judge and erased all her professional experience. They made it look like she was just a housewife who wanted to be a judge before the documents got to the council! Margrith wasn't sure who had done it, but she knew that many of her male colleagues did not want a woman to become a federal judge.

Margrith grew up in Henau, St Gallen, in a very political family. Her family talked openly about issues in the world around them, such as workers in their village who weren't paid enough, people who didn't have enough money to feed their families and the difficulties faced by the refugees from Austria and Germany in the aftermath of the Second World War. Margrith went to the meetings of the local democratic women's group and heard how women were discriminated against, and how they were fighting for equality.

As a teenager, on a school trip to Genoa, Italy, Margrith was inspired by the famous Staglieno cemetery, where she saw an inscription on one of the graves: 'Always active for the poor.' It was like a light bulb went off – she knew what she was going to do!

With that ideal in mind, Margrith studied law in Geneva and in Zurich, and researched PhD in Bern. She quickly found out that being a woman in a profession dominated by men was not going to be easy. At work, her colleagues did everything possible to get her to quit. They made her work in family law, because that's where they felt women should be. They wouldn't let her get new furniture for her office, because they assumed she wouldn't stay. They called her names because they didn't like her opinions. But she never let the bullies win. Not only did she work as a lawyer, but she published articles on the discrimination between men and women and the situation of the disabled. She would not let them silence her.

Despite somebody changing her papers, Margrith was elected as a federal judge in 1972. Disgusted that there was now a female judge, many fellow judges avoided her. One even refused to speak to her for five years. But to Margrith it didn't matter. She had studied law, become a lawyer and lecturer – all before women had the right to vote. Now she was the first female federal judge in Switzerland, and she had work to do.

'I spoke out in favour of women's equal pay in 1977.
That we still have no equal pay today makes me very angry.'

1971

Emilie Gourd

The Woman Who Fought for Women's Right to Vote

1879–1946

In 1912, a young Emilie Gourd stepped down from a podium in Geneva, having delivered a passionate speech on why women should have the right to vote – to thunderous applause. Flushed and proud, she knew that this was her calling. She would never stop fighting for women's rights.

From a young age, Emilie had bristled at inequalities between men and women. She wasn't allowed to study at university because she was a woman. She saw that women were paid much less than men for exactly the same job, and that, once married, a woman had to give up her job and her ambitions to serve her family. Emilie wondered: How could women ever change the laws in their favour if they weren't allowed to be part of political decisions? For meaningful change, women's suffrage was essential – they must have the right to vote!

When she became a suffragette, her father thought she was mad! Why couldn't his daughter just be a 'normal' woman? He wasn't the only person to think that way. Many people thought that the idea of women voting was ridiculous, and that women with power were dangerous. They said that Emilie was being selfish and abnormal. Some heckled her when she spoke, others wrote nasty letters.

None of this could stop Emilie. She wrote for newspapers and edited her magazine, *Le Mouvement Féministe*. She gathered signatures for petitions and talked to members of parliament. When she spoke at events across Switzerland and Europe, even the most stubborn doubters began to agree with her. Wherever she spoke, new suffragettes were born.

However, the journey to Swiss women's suffrage was long.

In 1919, the first European countries granted women the vote. Not Switzerland. Far from being discouraged, Emilie wrote, 'The idea is working!' and she kept trying.

In 1934, Swiss women still didn't have the right to vote. Emilie's passion did not lag. She wrote: 'Here we are, looking back at twenty-five years of fighting for women's suffrage. With melancholy? With discouragement? Not at all!'

She ran petitions, travelled from conference to conference, and wrote letters encouraging her fellow suffragettes all over the world.

In 1946, Switzerland was practically the only European country in which women still couldn't vote. Emilie was now sixty-seven years old and ill, but no less determined. She worked from her bed until the day she died.

Emilie stood at the front lines of the Swiss suffrage movement for thirty-six years. She died long before Switzerland finally granted women the vote in 1971. By then, Emilie would have been over ninety years old!

As Emilie knew, the right to vote was only the beginning. She inspired generations of women to keep fighting for their rights – and that idea is still working.

'The idea is working!'

Marie Grosholtz

The Woman Who Built a Wax Empire

1761–1850

Marie Grosholtz spent many nights collecting severed heads from the Madeleine Cemetery in Paris. She'd place them into a wicker basket, which she'd hold in her lap on the way back to her workshop. Before the heads could decay, she'd copy their likeness in wax. And these weren't just any heads, they were the heads of people who had been executed by guillotine.

Madame Tussaud was born Marie Grosholtz in Strasbourg, France to a Swiss mother and a German father. Her father died shortly before Marie's birth, so her mother returned to Switzerland, where she worked as housekeeper for Philippe Curtius in Bern. Philippe made human organs out of wax intended to teach anatomy to medical students, and he also made wax models of people's heads. Marie loved his work and insisted he teach her. She herself became a talented artist by the time she was seventeen. With Marie's help, Philippe modelled some of the most famous heads of the day, including Voltaire, Jean-Jacques Rousseau and Benjamin Franklin.

When Marie was nineteen, the French royal family invited her to the palace of Versailles to teach King Louis XVI's younger sister the art of wax modelling. Eight years later, the French Revolution broke out. Fed up with the royals, French citizens wanted more equality. They captured Louis XVI and his wife, Marie Antoinette, and sent them to the guillotine. Marie Grosholz was due to be executed as well. Her head was shaved in preparation for the guillotine, but she refused to let fright take over. Instead, Marie agreed to make wax death masks of the executed royals to 'prove' that she was not loyal to them – and this saved her own head.

Philippe died in 1794, leaving Marie his collection of wax figures. Soon after, she married François Tussaud, which turned out to be disastrous. By the time they had two sons, Marie recognised that François was squandering the money she earned from exhibiting her waxworks. So, in 1802 she took her show on the road, bringing her eldest son and a wagonful of wax figures on tour in Great Britain and Ireland. She survived shady business partners, shipwrecks and arson, and finally cut her husband off financially. In total, she travelled for twenty-seven years, displaying her rotating collection of fascinating waxworks. Finally, well into her seventies, Marie set up a permanent exhibition on London's Baker Street and let the crowds come to her. Madame Tussauds Wax Museum was born.

When Marie died, her sons prepared and displayed her death mask, including it in an ever-expanding exhibition that has become a worldwide phenomenon that still bears her name.

'[It] was her art to write history, but to write it in letters of blood!'
– Museum catalogue

Catherine Perregaux de Watteville

The Woman Who Spied for France

1645–1714

In December 1689, Bernese authorities burst into Catherine Perregaux de Watteville's home and dragged her from her bed. Accused of being a spy, she was imprisoned and interrogated. When she refused to name her accomplices, torturers hung her by her wrists with heavy stones on her ankles, wrapped her in copper wire until she bled and crushed her thumbs with a vice. Catherine cried out names, but they were mostly lies. This infuriated and confused the authorities.

Catherine had always infuriated and confused people. She didn't act like a woman of noble class. In fact, she didn't act like a woman at all. Catherine preferred shooting guns over sewing, equestrian challenges over embroidery. She was an expert rider and once won a bet by taming an untameable horse. She shot a man in the shoulder when he attacked her. She challenged another woman to a duel after being insulted. Catherine called herself an Amazon, and even had her portrait painted while wearing the garb of a warrior queen!

Catherine was also passionate about politics. Bern ruled the area of Vaud by force, and a large part of the population was pro-France. Catherine was one of them. She had big dreams of serving Louis XIV – the King of France, a glittering, majestic figure known as the Sun King – in his army or court.

But as Louis XIV's power spread across Europe, he was losing popularity in Switzerland. Pro-France supporters now risked punishment.

That didn't stop Catherine from living her dream. In early 1689, she finally found a way to serve Louis XIV. She became a spy for the French ambassador! She gathered political secrets from people she knew in the Bernese government and sent coded messages to him. Then one of her messages was intercepted. That's when Catherine was arrested and tortured.

She was sentenced to death and dragged to the scaffold, where an executioner readied a sword for her beheading. Her brother's carriage was already draped in black, set for a trip to the cemetery. But Catherine came from a well-respected family, and at the very last minute the city council changed her sentence: they banished her from Bernese territory forever.

Over the course of the following years, she compiled her memoirs and dedicated them to the Sun King. She had to dictate the text to her husband, because her tortured body and hands were too broken for her to write. But she did sign the work, proving the words were her own. And proving that while her torturers may have crushed her thumbs, they never crushed her spirit.

'I never had a penchant for coquetry ... but for grand and elevated things.'

Jrène Liggenstorfer

The Woman Who Drove Long-Haul Trucks

Born 1955

Jrène was being watched, again. This time it was five young men leaning against a fence, convinced she couldn't reverse her truck around the corner and into the loading bay. Even though her truck had 18 wheels and was as big as a blue whale, she easily proved them wrong.

Jrène first drove a truck when she was seventeen. Her friend, Ueli Liggenstorfer invited her to join him on a trip to Iran. It was too exciting to pass up! Along the way, Ueli asked her if she'd like to try driving. Jrène quickly learned how to manoeuvre the huge, eighteen-metre-long truck around tight corners in Turkey's remote mountain passes. She drove her first 2,000 kilometres on that trip – without a driver's license!

When Jrène returned home, she started nursing school, but she couldn't stop thinking about that road trip. She'd met so many interesting people and loved the sense of adventure. Determined to be a truck driver, she begged her father to sign the permission form so she could get a driver's license. Then, when he wasn't looking, she changed the form to say truck driver's licence instead!

In 1977, she became the first Swiss woman to drive long-haul trucks. She made the 10,000-kilometre round trip to Iran with Ueli eight times as a reserve driver. When Ueli got tired, Jrène drove. It was a dangerous route on remote, narrow and hazardous roads. Drivers faced mechanical breakdowns, wobbly bridges, sandstorms, theft, crazy taxi drivers and border delays. Nobody had mobile phones or GPS, so long-haul truck drivers stuck together in convoys, helping each other along the way. In the middle of the desert, Jrène's training as a nurse even saved a fellow driver's life. The man was burning up with a fever. Without ice to cool him down, Irene thinned alcohol with water, soaked a huge towel in it and covered him in the towel to bring his temperature down.

Jrène took her first solo trip as a long-haul trucker in 1979. But it didn't go according to plan. When she arrived at her destination in Germany, two angry American soldiers appeared out of the darkness. Jrène had accidently parked on an American army base.

Jrène started making regular solo trips from Germany to Italy. Over the years, she outsmarted the Italian Mafia trying to steal her truck and cargo, narrowly missed being hit by an avalanche, nearly had her truck blow up and dealt with all kinds of mechanical failures.

From 1990 to 1996, Jrène supported the charity 'Thun Helps Romania' by transporting medical supplies and clothing in her truck, the 'Green Angel', to Romania seventeen times. Her son Christian was two the first time he made the 5,000-kilometre round trip with her. Many of her friends also helped transport aid goods for free.

In 2019, Jrène retired. She had driven over a million kilometres in her career – that's farther than to the moon and back.

'Be curious and learn from everyone that you meet.'

N
W
E
S

Martina Hingis

The Woman Who Was #1 at Tennis for 209 weeks

Born 1980

Wimbledon, 1997. Sixteen-year-old Martina Hingis was ready. She knew that if she won this next game, she would be the youngest tennis champion in a century. To get there, she couldn't just be strong. She had to be smart. It wasn't just about hitting the ball over the net, it was about where the ball would land. She would make her opponent run around, chasing that ball, tiring her out. Martina knew exactly what to do.

Even before Martina had been born, her mother already had Martina's life planned out: she would be a tennis champion. Martina started playing tennis when she was just two years old. While growing up in Trübbach, St Gallen, she played sports for six hours a day – practising tennis for four hours – and spending the rest of that time biking, swimming and riding horses. Each sport exercised different parts of her body and brain.

Martina especially loved horseback riding. She didn't just ride horses. She fed them, cleaned them – and often came home very smelly. Spending so much time with the horses helped her understand them, and think about what she needed to do to be a better rider. And she has the exact same thinking with tennis. After every one of her matches, Martina would always look back and review every game to see how she could have done better.

At fourteen, Martina was already a tennis superstar. When she won Wimbledon in 1997, she made history. Whenever she played, her mixture of mental and physical strength allowed her to dominate the sport. She is still considered one of tennis's great legends.

Martina pushed herself hard as an athlete, which was very hard on her body. At twenty-two, she had to stop due to pain – she had surgery on the ligaments of both ankles, and afterwards was never able to get back to her best form. Yet, because she had so many other interests, she was never bored: 'I want to play tennis only for fun and concentrate more on horse riding and finish my studies.' She did return to competition until 2017, when she retired once and for all.

Today, Martina still plays tennis in her local club and exercises as much as she can. But instead of it being her main focus, she also spends a lot of time with her horses and her family, ready to become a champion of something new, running her brand-new riding stable in Bad Ragaz.

'I didn't have the same fitness or ability as the other girls, so I had to beat them with my mind.'

Angela Ziltener

The Woman Who Dives With Dolphins

Born 1980

When Angela was eleven, she gave a presentation at her school: 'Where do you see yourself when you are grown-up?' Angela stood up and declared, 'I see myself on a boat, researching dolphins.'

There was a moment's silence. Then everybody laughed. 'That's silly!' her teacher said. 'How would you study dolphins here in Switzerland?'

As a child in Würenlos, Angela walked her neighbours' dogs, looked after a pony and spent hours watching nature documentaries. She put her head underwater long before she could swim, wanting to find out what was beneath the surface – both in her bath and in the sea!

At dolphin parks, Angela witnessed the strength, power and grace of these intelligent mammals. She felt sad for the captive dolphins and desperately wanted to see them in the wild. Later, Angela studied biology and worked for the Walter Zoo near St Gallen. Whenever she could, she volunteered at whale-watching stations and animal shelters around the world.

Diving in the Red Sea in Egypt for the first time, Angela immediately saw that it was a paradise for dolphin research! She set herself up to earn money in Switzerland for half the year, and to live in Egypt for the other half. For over ten years, she dived with Indo-Pacific bottlenose dolphins (*Tursiops aduncus*), observing how they sleep (swimming in groups, one eye open, one eye closed), how they play and how they communicate with each other.

However, there was a big problem: dolphin tourism. More and more tourists flocked to the Red Sea to 'swim with dolphins'. Every day, hundreds of people would be taken out on boats, jump into the water and disturb the dolphins. Angela noticed how the dolphins' behaviour changed. Instead of sleeping until 2 or 3pm every day, they now woke up at 11am. They dived for longer, came up for air less often and swam in larger circles to avoid humans. The dolphins were scared and stressed. Angela saw how tourism was destroying the dolphins' home.

So, Angela set up a campaign to educate people about dolphins. She talked to tour organisers, tourists and schools to help them be more respectful of the environment. As a result, many tour providers adapted their activities to be more dolphin friendly. Angela also created Dolphin Watch Alliance, an organisation that aims to better understand and protect dolphins.

Angela advised the film teams for the BBC documentaries *Blue Planet II, Disney Nature Dolphin Reef* and *Diving With Dolphins*. In these films, you can see her researching dolphins – just like she always said she would.

'Trust in yourself. Explore your strengths and take action.'

Tina Turner

The Woman Who Is the Queen of Rock and Roll

Born 1939

In 1990, Tina Turner leaned over the railing of the Eiffel Tower and looked down on Paris hundreds of feet below. Now or never! She climbed over the railing in her spiky heels, held onto the metal girders and let go with one hand. She wasn't preparing to jump. She was doing a photoshoot for her new album *Foreign Affair* to celebrate her move to Europe … and she was having the time of her life.

Tina Turner was born Anna Mae Bullock, the third daughter of a poor family. Her mother abandoned the family, moving to St Louis when Anna was eleven. Her father left when she was thirteen, never to be seen again, so Anna and her sisters lived with their grandmother. Anna struggled in school, feeling 'not smart' most of the time. She eventually learned that she had dyslexia, which meant that her brain made it hard to read and do math.

Anna had a powerful singing voice. She sang at church, town picnics and in the local department store, where saleswomen threw coins to her. At sixteen, she moved in with her mother in St Louis. There, she met Ike Turner, a musician who recognised her talent immediately and knew she would earn him money. He transformed Anna Mae Bullock into Tina Turner, a singing and dancing phenomenon, and convinced her that marrying him would bring more success.

As Tina shot to stardom, Ike realised that fans were coming to see her – not him. So, he kept control of all the money, which kept her loyal to him – and unable to leave. He blamed Tina for his own lack of success and often hit her.

By 1976, Tina realised that there was no excuse for the abuse. She left with thirty-six cents in her pocket. One year later, she took control of her career by launching a solo concert tour.

Stardom became superstardom. Tina released hit albums, acted in films and became known as 'The Queen of Rock and Roll'. She set a Guinness World Record in 1988 for selling the most tickets ever for a single concert. In 1991, she was inducted into the Rock and Roll Hall of Fame.

Tina moved to Zurich in 1994 and fell in love with Switzerland. She applied for citizenship in 2013 and studied German for her citizenship interview, passing it with flying colours. She's called Switzerland home ever since.

Over the years, Tina has battled a stroke, cancer and kidney failure, but has fought back every time. The girl who entered the world unloved, survived a hellish marriage and often had to fight for her life battles on with a smile on her beautiful face and a will of steel that is bigger and more impressive than the Eiffel Tower.

'If you rise from the ashes, life will open up for you.'

Hélène Rey

The Woman Who Fought Back

1819–unknown

In 1847, Hélène Rey hit one neighbour with a stick, poured the contents of her chamber pot over the head of another and told off the village authorities. She had lost her professional certification and endured five years of cruel lies and name calling. Her life and career were ruined.

In 1842, Hélène was in her early twenties, happily unmarried and living alone by choice. She was independent at a time when women were expected to be submissive. That made people angry. Some told lies about her. Some even hated her. The prior – the head of the religious community – of the village of Val-d'Illiez was especially outraged by her choices. He decided to do something about it.

Hélène was learning to be a midwife so she could treat pregnant women and help them give birth. The prior wrote to the head of the midwifery program, requesting that Hélène be pulled from the training. He accused Hélène of skipping church, having a relationship with a married man, having secretly had children and even of killing a child! He could prove nothing except Hélène's lack of attendance at Mass, yet he expected his demand to be carried out. His request was denied.

Furious, the prior went to the state council with his complaints, insisting that Hélène not receive her certificate to practice midwifery. But the prior still didn't get his way.

Hélène finished her training and began to work as a midwife. In 1844, there was a change in political power. The prior approached the new council, once again demanding Hélène's certificate be taken away. The new government officials listened to him and agreed.

Now Hélène could no longer work as a midwife. The lies about her spread. The locals called her names and threatened to harm her. But she dug in her heels and demanded answers. When the rumours flew, Hélène said to her accusers, 'Prove it.'

In 1847, the local authorities put Hélène on trial, which lasted several months. Villagers continued to harass Hélène, and her frustration reached a boiling point. She fought with her neighbours and swore at authorities. Despite no evidence to support the prior's earlier complaints, the council refused to allow Hélène to work as a midwife. They wanted her to give up and go away.

But Hélène didn't go away, and she never gave up. In 1848, there was another change in government and Hélène brought her case to the new council. It paid off! Her certificate was returned to her and she was finally able to do the job she loved.

'Prove it.'

Angelika Kauffmann

The Woman Who Was a World-Famous Painter

1741–1807

Angelika packed up her oil painting of David Garrick, the famous British actor. His romantic poem about her could have ruined her career, but he looked gorgeous on canvas! She knew this portrait would help make her a superstar.

When the portrait arrived in London for exhibition in 1765, everyone wanted to see it. One art critic described her as 'a luminous wonder'. And so she sailed to the 'portrait capital of the world' to make a fortune.

Although Angelika had been painting portraits for noble Swiss families since she was just twelve, it was impossible for her to become a professional painter. Women couldn't go to art school. She couldn't even study the human body or draw nude models because it was taboo for a woman to view nudity. So how could she learn to paint?

She had to teach herself. For six years, Angelika worked from dawn to dusk, copying Raphael and other Italian Renaissance masters. Later, when she was hired to paint people, she made her clients appear more attractive than in real life. This made her very popular, especially with King Ferdinand of Naples, who everyone called 'King Big Nose' behind his back. He adored the smaller nose Angelika painted in his portrait.

There were 2,000 portrait painters in London in the 1760s, and most of them were men. Everyone thought men were better painters. Yet, Angelika's artwork was incredibly popular. After her arrival in London, Angelika wrote to her father, 'I have finished some portraits which are snapped up by everyone.' To keep up with demand, she once painted a client's face in just five hours – work that normally took days.

Angelika became one of Queen Charlotte's favourites and got even more work from the Queen's friends. She started painting tender scenes featuring women from history and mythology, which were so popular she decided to mass produce them. Working with engravers, she helped invent techniques to transfer her art onto dishware, furniture, fabric, wall decorations and prints that sold all over Europe and even as far away as China.

As a woman, Angelica was constantly threatened by scandal. When David Garrick published a love poem about her, she was lucky to have royal friends to protect her. The same was true when she married a man who'd lied about being a Swedish noble only to steal her money.

Everyone wanted Angelika's art in their homes, and she made sure they had it. She is one of the most successful women artists in history!

'The whole world is Angelika-mad!'
–The Danish Ambassador to London, 1781

Nadia Isler

The Woman Who Builds Bridges

Born 1976

When Nadia Isler first stepped into the United Nations Building in New York City in 2007, she felt like a tiny ant. As a Swiss diplomat, she represented Switzerland on many important matters. But she would be working with extremely powerful people like ambassadors and presidents. Would anyone listen to what she had to say?

Growing up in Geneva, Nadia had a lot of ideas about what she wanted to do when she was older. She wanted to travel, meet people, understand different cultures and – somehow – bring the different people of the world closer together.

Nadia found a way to do all of it! She became a diplomat representing Switzerland at the United Nations and to other governments. She chatted with ambassadors and presidents, but wasn't intimidated by them. Though it was scary at first, Nadia took part in discussions with even the most powerful people, and grew more confident with time. She had been worried that no one would listen to her. But instead she realised her job gave her a voice – and was in exactly the right place to help make sure people with very little power were heard. She focused on inequalities in the world, including the plight of migrants – people who move from one place to another – and women.

People migrate for many reasons. They might be forced to move, running from danger in their home country or they might simply be looking for a better life. They are often poor and face difficulties after they migrate. Their children don't always have food to eat, access to education or healthcare. In the end, despite wanting to improve their lives, they often find themselves in another terrible situation.

Women, too, may face serious difficulties. In many places in the world, women often don't have the same rights or protections as men, and they suffer the most from poverty and violence.

As a representative of Switzerland, Nadia was asked to work with different countries to speed up the discussion on migration and women in the United Nations, even creating a new UN agency – UN Women – in the process! This would make sure that the suffering of these vulnerable people would be heard and discussed by the very people who could help make their lives better.

Today, Nadia works for the United Nations and spends most of her time in Geneva so she can stay close to her children, because – as important as her work is – her children are important too. She continues to work and build bridges between people and ideas, bringing real and positive change to the world.

'When it feels like you are taking a step back, you may be making a huge leap forward!'

Manuela Oppikofer

The Woman Who Learned to Stop the Bullies

Born 1990

Every time Manuela Oppikofer tried to read or write, the letters would dance about in front of her eyes. She couldn't make any sense of it! Her uncle, a schoolteacher, grew frustrated and angry, calling her stupid and useless. Manuela knew that she wasn't stupid, but she couldn't work out what the problem was.

Manuela's father died when she was just one year old, and shortly afterwards her mother left Yaoundé, Cameroon to work in Switzerland. Aunts and uncles in Cameroon took turns looking after Manuela and her sister but they were very poor. If their mother couldn't send money to pay for food and school fees, the sisters went hungry and missed school.

When Manuela was ten, she and her sister finally joined their mother in Switzerland, the happiest day of their lives. Manuela knew that, at the very least, she would always be close to her mother now.

However, life in Lausanne, Switzerland, wasn't easy. Manuela was one of only three black students in her school. She was bullied because of her skin colour, and she still couldn't read or write. Finally, a teacher recognised that Manuela had dyslexia. Manuela was not stupid; her brain just worked differently. With the right help, her reading and writing quickly improved.

Manuela loved fashion, so after school, she looked for an apprenticeship in a clothing store. She sent dozens of applications, but didn't get invited to one interview. When she finally did find work as a shop assistant, one of her colleagues called her names and spread lies about her.

Manuela had had enough of being bullied! She joined the Swiss Army and trained for six months, the only woman alongside ninety-one men. Through learning how to handle weapons, treat injuries and stand up to her male colleagues, Manuela's body and mind got stronger, and she became more confident.

Then, Manuela signed up for the Miss Earth contest, a beauty pageant that aims to change the world for the better. Manuela won! She was crowned Miss Earth Switzerland 2016, and became an ambassador for MyBluePlanet and Plan International Switzerland. With the Swiss Red Cross, she accompanied a young girl in Ghana through a life-changing eye operation. Because of her army training, Manuela could even assist with the operation.

From then on, Manuela wanted to be her own boss. Building on the skills and knowledge gained as Miss Earth Switzerland, she set up a coaching agency for models. Her agency helps other women to be themselves and to celebrate their beauty. Running your own business isn't always easy, but Manuela keeps going, building her own life the way she wants it to be.

'Life can be a fight, and Prince Charming doesn't exist! Always look ahead, and continue to fight for what you want.'

Franziska Dosenbach

The Woman Who Started a Shoe Empire

1832–1917

On 6 May 1870, Franziska Dosenbach was returning home from a shoe-shopping trip when she told her servant to speed up the horses. She was about to give birth to her twelfth child ... and then she needed to get back to work.

Anna Maria Franziska Buchmann was born in a small village, but didn't live there long. Her father died when she was young and her mother remarried, moving the family to Bremgarten, Aargau. Franziska was sent to study at the nearby *Töchterinstitut Ruepp*, which was known for teaching its students the art of good housekeeping, French and music. Franziska loved her music lessons, but was especially interested in *Strohgeflecht* (straw plaiting), which is the craft of fashioning straw into useful articles, such as hats, caps and bags, as well as decorations for trimming hats and shoes.

After finishing school, Franziska worked for a company as a dealer, buying plaited straw items produced by homeworkers. By the time she was twenty-one years old, Franziska was known all over Bremgarten for her business sense – and her beauty. She got more than a few marriage proposals. In 1853, she chose Kaspar Dosenbach, the only saddle maker in Bremgarten.

In 1865, Franziska visited a trade fair in Zurich and saw stands displaying factory-made shoes from Germany. The prices were super cheap! Franziska grabbed several dozen pairs and headed back to Bremgarten, setting up a shoe-filled shelf at the saddlery. In those days, factory-made shoes were a relatively new concept and people were not very quick to buy them. However, Franziska was wasn't about to give up on what she thought was a good idea. She could sell those shoes.

Franziska listened for news of shoe manufacturers selling out their stock or going out of business. She bought their shoes and took them to trade fairs all over Switzerland. Starting in 1875, she visited trade fairs at sixteen different Swiss cities and towns – attending most of them several times per year – and sold lots and lots of shoes. By that time, Franziska had thirteen children, was helping Kaspar in the saddlery and managing this booming new shoe business.

The saddlery/shoe shop in Bremgarten had become too small for selling both saddles and shoes. Franziska bought a building in Zurich and had it remodelled into a beautiful shoe store. *Schuhwarenhaus Dosenbach* was born.

Even after Kaspar died in 1877, Franziska didn't slow down. Ever the businesswoman, she opened a new store in Baden in 1878, and then just kept going. By the time she died, she'd built a shoe empire of seventeen stores all across Switzerland, earning her the nickname *Finken Fränzi* ('Slippers Fränzi'). The Swiss shoe business hasn't been the same since.

Susanna Orelli-Rinderknecht

The Woman Who Made Coffee Shops Cool

1845–1939

For years, Susanna Orelli-Rinderknecht took part in groups that preached, 'Alcohol kills!' and 'Beer makes you fat, dumb and lazy!' She handed out brochures warning of the dangers of drinking, illustrated by drawings of the devil lurking in a bottle of liquor. But in 1894, Susanna decided to try something different. She decided to make coffee.

Growing up, Susanna had witnessed the destructive effects of alcohol. There was the drunk man who'd set her family's barn on fire. The inebriated neighbor who shot himself. Her intoxicated stepbrother who fell from a carriage and died. Then, when her sister was briefly put into a mental institution, Susanna came face-to-face with many of the patients who were there due to alcoholism (an addiction to drinking alcohol). She saw how heavy drinking could lead to violence, poverty, accidents, depression and even death.

At the time, people drank on average much more than we do today. While it was mostly men who drank too much, it was also a huge problem for women. Drunk men were more likely to hit their wives or children, or to abandon their families. There was such a problem with drunkenness that 'temperance' or 'abstinence' organisations were started, demanding that people drink less, or not at all.

Susanna was a part of these organisations. However, she was soon frustrated at their lack of success. Susanna didn't believe that alcohol needed to be banned, but that there simply needed to be better alternatives to taverns and drinking – places where people could meet up and discuss the day over something other than a mug of beer. Unlike today, it wasn't common to meet in a café for hot chocolate or coffee.

Susanna got a group together and opened a small coffeehouse where guests could get non-alcoholic drinks and low-cost meals. It was an instant success, but Susanna wanted to do even more.

She founded what would be called the Zurich Women's Union for Non-Alcoholic Restaurants (ZFV). The ZFV intended to open larger cafés, but didn't have the money. So, they held a huge bazaar selling homemade cakes and tickets for evening entertainment. In two days, they made over 17,000Fr – that's about 170,000Fr in today's money! Cafés, restaurants, hotels – the ZFV continued to open more places in Zurich and beyond, offering alcohol-free options to the public. Susanna's alternative to fighting alcoholism was so successful that, in 1919, the University of Zurich gave her an honorary doctorate for her 'accomplishments in the field of public health and welfare'. Though no longer entirely alcohol-free, the ZFV still exists today as a hotel and catering company, serving all of Switzerland. So, the next time you order hot chocolate, lift your cup to toast Susanna!

'Guests of every class should feel comfortable with us and be served with the same attention as one would serve friends.'

Iris Bohnet

The Woman Who Elevates Women

Born 1966

Harvard University students at the Kennedy School of Government, half of them women, walked past many portraits of important leaders on their way to class every day. Not one painting depicted a woman … until the day a couple of professors, including Iris Bohnet, helped change that.

Iris grew up in Lucerne but paid attention to the whole world. One of the things that upset her most was inequality. She felt everyone should be treated equally and wanted to do something about it. When Iris went to university, she discovered her passion for behavioural economics – studying how people make decisions, how they make mistakes and why they treat each other unfairly.

Starting in 2007, as the Director of Harvard's Women and Public Policy Program, Iris researched how companies, schools and governments can build better societies by avoiding unconscious gender bias — treating and rewarding women and men differently without realising they are doing so.

Iris's research revealed that we all unknowingly treat people differently because of their looks. That's very hard to change, whether you're a child or an executive at a big company. Iris herself experienced it when she took her son to day-care for the first time. She was shocked to discover her own bias towards the male teacher because a *man* didn't fit her idea of what a preschool teacher should look like.

But one study caught her attention. In the 1970s, major US orchestras discovered that, by adding a simple curtain during auditions, they could just listen to the music rather than judging the musicians based on their looks. Not only did they recruit more talented musicians, but the fraction of female musicians grew from 5% to 35%.

Iris realised simple solutions like this could be used to remove bias from the workplace and schools. It's very difficult to change how we think, but it's easy to change our environment. It starts with how a job is advertised. If a company wants to attract women and men equally, they should avoid describing the preferred candidate as 'competitive' because that could discourage women from applying. Removing names from job applications helps managers focus on the person's qualifications, not their gender. Using these and other techniques, Iris helped increase the number of women in leadership positions within a very short amount of time.

Iris also found that seeing is believing. Seeing women in leadership, whether in business or politics, not only inspires girls, but changes what people believe is possible or normal. Thanks to Iris and her colleagues, many organisations, including Harvard, have made a simple change: hanging up more portraits of female role models. It's had a huge impact.

Cécile Biéler-Butticaz

The Woman Who Was the First Female Engineer in Switzerland

1884–1966

When she graduated from the Lausanne engineering school, Cécile Biéler-Butticaz knew she was lucky. Unique even. Cécile had been able to enter a professional world that was, for the most part, closed to women. But Cécile didn't want to be unique or lucky. She wanted all women to be able to do what she had done. Yet those opportunities didn't exist for everyone. Cécile would have to create them.

Growing up, Cécile was well educated and interested in technology. Her father was an engineer – someone who builds or designs engines, machines or structures like bridges or tunnels – and Cécile wanted to be one too. With her father's support, she enrolled in the *École d'ingénieurs* in Lausanne, where she studied electrical engineering. In 1907, she became the first Swiss woman to graduate with an engineering degree.

Cécile knew the only way women could move forward was if they supported each other. That meant using her success to help others. So, only two years after graduating, she started her own engineering company and decided to hire only female engineers!

In 1910, Cécile married another engineer and continued to work on many different projects. One of the biggest was the second tube of the Simplon Tunnel – a railway tunnel of over twenty kilometres dug through the Alps connecting Switzerland to Italy.

Engineering wasn't the only thing that interested Cécile. She was also a devoted mother and a writer. At the time, some people believed the brains of highly educated women were so deteriorated from intellectual thought that it ruined any possibility they could be good mothers! Cécile proved them wrong. She raised three children – with love – and regularly wrote scientific articles for the youth section of the *Gazette de Lausanne*. She also wrote poetry books, books on engineering and books on how to have a happy home. Plus, she regularly wrote opinion pieces for the newspaper. She pretty much had an opinion on everything!

But Cécile's biggest goal was always to help women advance both professionally and personally, and she was involved in numerous groups for the cause. Even at age sixty-five, Cécile helped set up the Lausanne chapter of an international women's group called the Soroptimists. The group brought women together and taught important leadership and practical skills to equip them for a successful professional life.

Cécile was a force for women everywhere – because of who she was, what she'd done and what she helped others to achieve.

'... she was a true feminist.'
– Philippe Biéler, her grandson

Eveline Hasler

The Woman Who Rescues People from the Dustbin of History

Born 1933

As a child, Eveline Hasler heard tales of a woman named Anna Göldin who, 200 years earlier, had been accused of witchcraft. Anna was tried in a court in Glarus, declared guilty and, in 1782, was the last woman to be executed as a witch in all of Switzerland.

Eveline was curious about this mysterious 'witch'. Anna Göldin had worked as a maid in Eveline's town, but when Eveline asked her teachers and family about her, everyone rapidly changed the subject. Eveline felt as if people would rather brush over that dark part of her town's history.

When Eveline was nine, her parents divorced. It was 1942, and divorce was unheard of in the tiny Canton of Glarus – a terrible scandal! People whispered behind Eveline's back and, in an instant, Eveline went from being a 'normal' child to 'the child without a mother'. She was an outsider, which was hard, but it also gave her the freedom to act differently from everyone else. It also made her fascinated by other outsiders, such as the mysterious witch of Glarus.

Eveline left Glarus to study history and psychology in Freiburg and Paris, became a teacher, and wrote over forty successful children's books. However, she never forgot Anna Göldin, and eventually decided to write about her.

Anna Göldin, the Last Witch, was Eveline's first historical biography. Through vivid details, she brought history to life and captured the thoughts and experiences of Anna Göldin for the reader to feel. The book was an instant hit. Eveline had broken a huge taboo, uncovering the terrible and uncomfortable history of witch hunts in Switzerland, initiating discussions and inspiring a whole new generation of historians. Because of Eveline's work, the courts in Glarus eventually reopened Anna Göldin's case and officially announced her innocent of all crimes – 200 years after her death!

Over the course of her life, Eveline has uncovered the fascinating stories of dozens more amazing people who would have otherwise been forgotten: Emily Kempin-Spyri, Switzerland's first female lawyer; Rösy Fäh, a Swiss woman who protected hundreds of Jewish children from the Nazis in France; Julie Bondeli, the centre of cultural life in Bern in the eighteenth century; Henry Dunant, the founder of the International Committee of the Red Cross; and many, many more.

Eveline never shies away from uncomfortable social truths or difficult subjects. To this day, all of her stories have one thing in common. The protagonist is always an outsider, like Eveline herself once was: somebody who dared to be different.

'Nothing fascinates me as much as people who really lived. Because nothing is as fantastical as reality.'

One More Amazing Person

As we've seen in this book, everybody is amazing in their very own way. Think about what makes you amazing and then write your own story here.

Name: ______________________

Date of birth: ______________________

The Person Who: ______________________

My story: ______________________

One More Amazing Person
Draw Your Own Portrait

Thank You

The authors and publisher would like to thank the following sponsors, whose generosity made this book possible:

BPW SWITZERLAND
Business & Professional Women
CLUB LAKE GENEVA

HSK English

1971 CH 2021
50 Jahre Frauenstimmrecht

KPMG

CTC
Resourcing Solutions

salt
CONSULTING AND COMMUNICATIONS

ELABASEL
The Swiss British School of Basel

SIS
Swiss International School

EXPLORIT
VOLKETSWIL • ZÜRICH

EY
Building a better working world

Acknowledgements

We would like to thank all the inspiring women in this book, both from the past and present. Our special thanks to those who took the time to sit with us for an interview … or many interviews.

The authors and illustrator also wish to thank the following people for their generous help and support in the creation of this book:

Gerd, Marlow, and Savannah Theurer
Julia and Andy Nigg
Ian, Robin, Hannah, Luca Steed Lehmann
Asier Aguirre
Laurent Hayoz

Laura Burge
Jeanne Darling
Gaby Dickenmann
Renate Diemand
Deborah Egger-Biniores, MSW
Silvia Feniello
Thomas Fischer, Dr. Phil
Paula Freedman
Louise Gooding
Kristine Greenaway
Katarina and Hans-Jörg Gsteiger
Richard Harvell
Katie Hawks
Genevieve Hayoz
Ludwig Heuss
Tracy Hope
Jeannine Johnson Maia
William A. Jordan III
Thomas und Bettina Keller
(Hotel Sunnehüsi, Krattigen)
Simone Kick
Sabine Lorenz
Joy Manné
Sandra Nickel
Elisabeth Norton
Pierre-Henri Parisod
Susan Platt
Kali Resler
Franziska Rogger
Marlene Roth
Monica Rull
Lais Stephan
Harriet Truscott
Nic Ulmi
Melanie Welfing
Ellen Yeomans
Mathilde Girardin Zufferey

Geneva Writers Group
Society of Children's Book Writers
and Illustrators

All who researched these amazing Swiss women before us and made it possible to find information about their lives.